Fashion

Anna Cora Mowatt

Dedication

To WALTER WATTS, ESQ.,

ONE of the most liberal supporters of the Drama, whose desire to elevate and purify it—whose appreciation and patronage of its humblest as, well as highest talent—whose liberality and consideration to all with whom the profession connects him—and whose efforts to establish harmony amongst them, while he promotes the interest of all, are beyond eulogium, the Comedy of "FASHION" is respectfully dedicated, with the grateful acknowledgments of

ANNA CORA MOWATT.

PREFACE

THE Comedy of Fashion was intended as a good-natured satire upon some of the follies incident to a new country, where foreign dross sometimes passes for gold, while native gold is cast aside as dross; where the vanities rather than the virtues of other lands are too often imitated, and where the stamp of fashion gives currency even to the coinage of vice.

The reception with which the Comedy was favoured proves that the picture represented was not a highly exaggerated one.

It was first produced at the Park Theatre, New York, in March, 1845.

The splendid manner in which the play was put upon the stage, and the combined efforts of an extremely talented company, ensured it a long continued success. It was afterwards received with the same indulgence in all the principal cities of the United States, for which the authoress is doubtless indebted to the proverbial gallantry of Americans to a countrywoman.

A. C. M.

London, January, 1850.

Dramatis Personae

- Adam Trueman, a Farmer from Catteraugus.
- Count Jolimaitre, a fashionable European Importation.
- Colonel Howard, an Officer in the U. S. Army.
- Mr. Tiffany, a New York Merchant.
- T. Tennyson Twinkle, a Modern Poet.
- Augustus Fogg, a Drawing Room Appendage.
- Snobson, a rare species of Confidential Clerk.
- Zeke, a colored Servant.
- Mrs. Tiffany, a Lady who imagines herself fashionable.
- Prudence, a Maiden Lady of a certain age.
- Millinette, a French Lady's Maid.
- Gertrude, a Governess.
- Seraphina Tiffany, a Belle.
- Ladies and Gentlemen of the Ball Room.

Costumes

- Adam Trueman.—First Dress: A farmer's rough overcoat, coarse blue trousers, heavy boots, broad-brimmed hat, dark coloured neckerchief, stout walking stick, large bandanna tied loosely around his neck.—Second dress: Dark grey old-fashioned coat, black and yellow waistcoat, trousers as before.—Third dress: Black old-fashioned dress cost, black trousers, white vest, white cravat.

- Count Jolimaitre.—First dress: Dark frock coat, light blue trousers, patent leather boots, gay coloured vest and scarf, profusion of jewellery, light overcoat.—Second dress: Full evening dress; last scene, travelling cap and cloak.

- Mr. Tiffany.—First dress: Dark coat, vest, and trousers.—Second dress: Full evening dress.

- Mr. Twinkle.—First dress: Green frock coat, white vest and trousers, green and white scarf.—Second dress: Full evening dress.

- Mr. Fogg.—First dress: Entire black suit.—Second dress: Fall evening dress, same colour.

- Snobson. —First dress: Blue Albert coat with brass buttons, yellow vest, red and black cravat, broad plaid trousers.—Second dress: Evening dress.

- Col. Howard.—First dress: Blue undress frock coat and cap, white trousers.—Second dress: Full military uniform.

- Zeke.—Red and blue livery, cocked hat, &c.

- Mrs. Tiffany.—First dress: Extravagant modern dress.—Second dress: Hat, feathers, and mantle, with the above.-Third dress: Morning dress.-Fourth dress: Rich ball dress.

- Serafina.—First dress: Rich modern dress, lady's tarpaulin on one side of head.—Second dress: Morning dress.—Third dress:

Handsome ball dress, profusion of ornaments and flowers.-Fourth dress: Bonnet and mantle.

- Gertrude.—First dress: White muslin.—Second dress: Ball dress, very simple.

- Millinette.—Ladies Maid's dress, very gay.

- Prudence.—Black satin, very narrow in the skirt, tight sleeves, white muslin apron, neckerchief of the same, folded over bosom, old-fashioned cap, high top and broad frill, and red ribbons.

Exits and entrances

R. means Right; L., Left; R. 1 E., Right First Entrance; 2 H., Second Entrance; D. F., Door in the Flat.

Relative positions

R. means Right; L., Left: C., Centre; R. C., Right of Centre: L. C., Left of Centre.

The reader is supposed to be on the Stage facing the Audience.

Fashion

PROLOGUE[1]

(Enter a Gentleman, reading a Newspaper.)

"'Fashion, a Comedy.' I'll go; but stay—
Now I read farther, 'tis a native play!
Bah! homemade calicoes are well enough,
But homemade dramas *must* be stupid stuff.
Had it the *London* stamp, 'twould do—but then,
For plays, we lack the manners and the men!"

Thus speaks one critic. Here's another's creed:—
"'Fashion!' What's here? (*Reads.*) It never can succeed!
What! from a woman's pen? It takes a man
To write a comedy—no woman can."

Well, sir, and what say you, and why that frown?
His eyes uprolled, he lays the paper down:—
"Here! take," he says, "the unclean thing away!
'This tainted with the notice of a play!"

But, sir!—but, gentlemen!—you, sir, who think
No comedy can flow from native ink,&mdash
Are we such *perfect* monsters, or such *dull*,
That Wit no traits for ridicule can cull?
Have we no follies here to be redressed?
No vices gibbeted? no crimes confessed?
"But then a female hand can't lay the lash on!"
How know you that, sir, when the theme is Fashion?

And now, come forth, thou man of sanctity!
How shall I venture a reply to thee?
The Stage—what is it, though beneath thy ban,
But a daguerreotype of life and man?
Arraign poor human nature, if you will,
But let the Drama have her mission still;
Let her, with honest purpose, still reflect
The faults which keeneyed Satire may detect.
For there *be* men who fear not an hereafter,
Yet tremble at the hell of public laughter!

Friends, from these scoffers we appeal to you!
Condemn the false, but O, applaud the true.
Grant that *some* wit may grow on native soil
And art's fair fabric rise from woman's toil.
While we exhibit but to *reprehend*
The social voices, 'tis for *you* to mend!

1.   By Epes Sargent (1813-80), Boston author and journalist, and friend of the Mowatt family. He had suggested that she write the play, and later helped with some of the technical details of its composition.

Fashion

ACT I

SCENE I

A splendid Drawing Room in the House of Mrs. Tiffany. Open folding door C. F., discovering a Conservatory. On either side glass windows down to the ground. Doors on R. and L. U. E. Mirror, couches, ottomans, a table with albums, &c., beside it an arm chair. Millinette R. dusting furniture, &c., Zeke L. in a dashing livery, scarlet coat, &c.

Zeke

Dere's a coat to take de eyes ob all Broadway! Ah! Missy, it am de fixins dat make de natural born gemman. A libery for ever! Dere's a pair ob insuppressibles :to 'stonish de colored population.

Millinette.

Oh, oui, Monsieur Zeke (very politely). I not comprend one word he say ! (aside.)

Zeke

I tell 'ee what, Missy, I'm 'stordinary glad to find dis a bery 'spectabul like :situation! Now as you've made de acquaintance ob dis here family, and dere you've :had a supernumerary advantage ob me—seeing dat I only receibed my appointment :dis morning. What I wants to know is your publicated, opinion, privately :expressed, ob de domestic circle.

Mil.

You mean vat espèce, vat kind of personnes are Monsieur and Madame Tiffany? Ah! Monsieur is not de same ting as Madame,—not at all.

Fashion

Zeke

Well, I s'pose he aint altogether.

Mil.

Monsieur is man of business,—Madame is lady of fashion. Monsieur make de money,—Madame spend it. Monsieur nobody at all,—Madame everybody altogether. Ah! Monsieur Zeke, de money is all dat is necessaire in country to make one lady of fashion. Oh! it is quite oder ting in la belle France!

Zeke

A bery lucifer explanation. Well, now we've disposed ob de heads ob de family, who come next?

Mil.

First, dere is Mademoiselle Seraphina Tiffany. Mademoiselle is not at all one proper personne. Mademoiselle Seraphina is one coquette. Dat is not de mode in la belle France; de ladies, dere, never learn la coquetrie until dey do get one husband.

Zeke

I tell 'ee what, Missy, I disreprobate dat proceeding altogeder!

Mil.

Vait! I have not tell you all la famille yet. Dere is Ma'mselle Prudence—Madame's sister, one very bizarre personne. Den dere is Ma'mselle Gertrude, but she not anybody at all; she only teach Mademoiselle Seraphina la musique.

Zeke

Well now, Missy, what's your own special defunctions?

Fashion

Mil.

I not understand, Monsieur Zeke.

Zeke

Den I'll amplify. What's de nature ob your exclusive services?

Mil.

Ah, oui! je comprend. I am Madame's femme de chambre—her lady's maid, Monsieur Zeke. I teach Madame les modes de Paris, and Madame set de fashion for all New York. You see, Monsieur Zeke, dat it is me, moi-meme, dat do lead de fashion for all de American beau monde!

Zeke

Yah! yah! yah! I hab de idea by de heel. Well now, p'raps you can 'lustrify my officials?

Mil.

Vat you will have to do? Oh! much tings, much tings. You vait on de table,—you tend de door,—you clean de boots,—you run de errands,—you drive de carriage,—you rub de horses,—you take care of de flowers, —you carry de water,—you help cook de dinner,— you wash de dishes,—and den you always remember to do everyting I tell you to!

Zeke

Wheugh, am dat all?

Mil.

All I can tink of now. To-day is Madame's day of reception, and all her grand friends do make her one petite visit. You mind run fast ven de bell do ring.

Zeke

Run? If it wasn't for dese superfluminous trimmings, I, tell 'ee what, Missy, I'd run—

Mrs. Tiffany.

(outside) Millinette!

Mil.

Here comes Madame! You better go, Monsieur Zeke.

Zeke

Look ahea, Massa Zeke, doesn't dis open rich! (aside).

[Exit Zeke, L.

Enter Mrs. Tiffany R., dressed in the most extravagant height of fashion.

Mrs. Tif.

Is everything in order, Millinette? Ah! very elegant, very elegant indeed! There is a jenny-says-quoi look about this furniture,—an air of fashion and gentility perfectly bewitching. Is there not, Millinette?

Mil.

Oh, oui, Madame!

Mrs. Tif.

But where is Miss Seraphina? It is twelve o'clock; our visitors will be pouring in, and she has not made her appearance. But I hear that nothing is more fashionable than to keep people waiting.—None but vulgar persons pay any attention to punctuality. Is it not so, Millinette?

Mil.

Quite comme il faut.—Great personnes always do make little personnes wait, Madame.

Mrs. Tif.

This mode of receiving visitors only upon one specified day of the week is a most convenient custom! It saves the trouble of keeping the house continually in order and of being always dressed. I flatter myself that I was the first to introduce it amongst the New York ee-light. You are quite sure that it is strictly a Parisian mode, Millinette?

Mil.

Oh, oui, Madame; entirely mode de Paris.

Mrs. Tif.

This girl is worth her weight in gold (aside). Millinette, how do you say arm-chair in French?

Mil.

Fauteuil, Madame.

Mrs. Tif.

Fo-tool! That has a foreign—an out-of-the-wayish sound that is perfectly charming—and so genteel! There is something about our American words decidedly vulgar. Fowtool! how refined. Fowtool! Arm-chair! what a difference!

Mil.

Madame have one charmante pronunciation. Fow-tool! (mimicking aside) charmante, Madame

Mrs. Tif.

Do, you think so, Millinette? Well, I believe I have. But a woman of refinement and of fashion can always accommodate herself to everything foreign! And a week's study of that invaluable work—"French without a Master," has made me quite at home in the court language of of Europe! But where is the new valet? I'm rather sorry that he is black, but to obtain a white American for a domestic is almost impossible; and they call this a free country! What did you say was the name of this new servant, Millinette?

Mil.

He do say his name is Monsieur Zeke.

Mrs. Tif.

Ezekiel, I suppose. Zeke! Dear me, such a vulgar name will compromise the dignity of the whole family. Can you not suggest something more aristocratic, Millinette? Something French!

Mil.

Oh, oui, Madame; Adolph is one very fine name.

Mrs. Tif.

A-dolph! Charming! Ring the bell, Millinette! (Millinette rings the bell). I will change his name immediately, besides giving him a few directions.

[Enter Zeke, L. U. H. Mrs. Tiffany addresses him with great dignity.

Your name, I hear, is Ezekiel.—I consider it too plebeian an appellation to be uttered in my presence. In future you are called A-dolph. Don't reply,—never interrupt me when I am speaking. A-dolph, as my guests arrive, I desire that you will inquire the name of every person, and then announce it in a loud, clear tone. That is the fashion in Paris.

[Millinette retires up the stage.

Fashion

Zeke

Consider de office discharged, Missus. [speaking very loudly.

Mrs. Tif.

Silence! Your business is to obey and not to talk.

Zeke

I'm dumb, Missus!

Mrs. Tif.

(pointing up stage) A-dolph, place that fowtool behind me.

Zeke

(looking about him) I hab'nt got dat far in de dictionary yet. No matter, a genus gets his learning by nature.

[takes up the table and places it behind Mrs. Tiffany, then expresses in dumb show great satisfaction. Mrs. Tiffany, as she goes to sit, discovers the mistake.

Mrs. Tif.

You dolt! Where have you lived not to know that fow-tool is the French for arm-chair ? What ignorance ! Leave the room this instant.

[Mrs. Tiffany draws forward an arm-chair and sits. Millinette comes forward suppressing her merriment at Zeke's mistake and removes the table.

Zeke

Dem's de defects ob not having a libery education.

[Exit L. U. H.

[Prudence peeps in, R. U. E.

Pru.

I wonder if any of the fine folks have come yet. Not a soul,—I knew they hadn't. There's Betsy all alone (walks in). Sister Betsy!

Mrs. Tif.

Prudence! how many times have I desired you to call me Elizabeth? Betsy is the height of vulgarity.

Pru.

Oh! I forgot. Dear me, how spruce we do look here, to be sure,—everything in first rate style now, Betsy.

[Mrs. T. looks at her angrily.

Elizabeth I mean. Who would have thought, when you and I were sitting behind that little mahogany-colored counter, in Canal Street, making up flashy hats and caps—

Mrs. Tif.

Prudence, what do you mean? Millinette, leave the room.

Mil.

R. Oui, Madame.

[Millinette pretends to arrange the books upon a side table, but lingers to listen.

Pru.

But I always predicted it,—I always told you so, Betsy,—I always said you were destined to rise above your station!

Mrs. Tif.

Prudence! Prudence! have I not told you that—

Pru.

No, Betsy, it was I that told you, when we used to buy our silks and ribbons of Mr. Antony Tiffany—"talking-Tony," you know we used to call him, and when you always put on the finest bonnet in our shop to go to his,—and when you staid so long smiling and chattering with him, I always told you that something would grow out of it—and didn't it?

Mrs. Tif.

Millinette, send Seraphina here instantly. Leave the room.

Mil.

Oui, Madame. So dis Americaine lady of fashion vas one milliner? Oh, vat a fine country for les merchandes des modes! I shall send for all my relation by de next packet ! (aside).

[Exit Millinette R. W. U. E.

Mrs. Tif.

Prudence! never let me hear you mention this subject again. Forget what we have been, it is enough to remember that we are of the upper ten thousand!

[Prudence goes up L. C. and sits down.

Enter Seraphina R. U. E., very extravagantly dressed.

Mrs. Tif.

How bewitchingly you look, my dear! Does Millinette say that that head dress is strictly Parisian?

Seraphina R.

Oh, yes, Mamma, all the rage! They call it a lady's tarpaulin, and it is the exact pattern of one worn by the Princess Clementina at the last court ball.

Mrs. Tif.

L. Now, Seraphina my dear, don't be too particular in your attentions to gentlemen not eligible. There is Count Jolimaitre, decidedly the most fashionable foreigner in town,—and so refined,—so much accustomed to associate with the first nobility in his own country that he can hardly tolerate the vulgarity of Americans in general. You may devote yourself to him. Mrs. Proudacre is dying to become acquainted with him. By the by, if she or her daughters should happen to drop in, be sure you don't introduce them to the Count. It is not the fashion in Paris to introduce—Millinette told me so.

Enter Zeke, L. U. E.

Zeke

(in a very loud voice) Mister T. Tennyson Twinkle!

Mrs. Tif.

Show him up.

[Exit Zeke L.

Pru.

I must be running away! [going.

Mrs. Tif.

Mr. T. Tennyson Twinkle—a very literary young man and a sweet poet! It is all the rage to patronize poets! Quick, Seraphina, hand me that magazine.—Mr. Twinkle writes for it.

[Seraphina hands the magazine, Mrs. T. seats herself in an arm-chair and opens the book.

Pru.

(returning L.) There's Betsy trying to make out that reading without her spectacles.

[takes a pair of spectacles out of her pocket and hands them to Mrs. Tiffany.

There, Betsy, I know, you were going to ask for them. Ah! they're a blessing when one is growing old!

Mrs. Tif.

What do you mean, Prudence? A woman of fashion never grows old! Age is always out of fashion.

Pru.

Oh. dear! what a delightful thing it is to be fashionable.

[Exit Prudence, R. U E. Mrs. Tiffany resumes her seat.

Enter Twinkle, L. (salutes Seraphina.)

Twin.

Fair Seraphina! the sun itself grows dim, unless you aid his light and shine on him!

Sera.

Ah! Mr. Twinkle, there is no such thing as answering you.

Twin.

(looks around and perceives Mrs. Tiffany) The "New Monthly Vernal Galaxy." Reading my verses by all that's charming! Sensible woman! I won't interrupt her. (aside).

Mrs. Tif.

(rising and coming forward) Ah! Mr. Twinkle, is that you? I was perfectly abimé at the perusal of your very distingué verses.

Twin.

I am overwhelmed, Madam. Permit me (taking the magazine). Yes, they do read tolerably. And you must take into consideration, ladies, the rapidity with which they were written. Four minutes and a half by the stop watch! The true test of a poet is the velocity with which he composes. Really they do look very prettily, and they read tolerably—quite tolerably—very tolerably, —especially the first verse. (reads) "To Seraphina T—."

Sera.

Oh! Mr. Twinkle!

Twin.

(reads) "Around my heart" —

Mrs. Tif.

How touching! Really, Mr. Twinkle, quite tender!

Twin.

(recommencing) "Around my heart" —

Mrs. Tif.

Oh, I must tell you, Mr. Twinkle! I heard the other day that poets were the aristocrats of literature. That's one reason I like them, for I do dote on all aristocracy!

Twin.

Oh, Madam, how flattering! Now pray lend me your ears! (reads) "Around my heart thou weavest" —

Sera.

R. That is such a sweet commencement, Mr. Twinkle!

Twin.

L. I wish she wouldn't interrupt me! (aside) (reads) "Around my heart thou weavest a spell" —

Mrs. Tif.

C. Beautiful! But excuse me one moment, while I say a word to Seraphina! Don't be too affable, my dear! Poets are very ornamental appendages to the drawing room, but they are always as poor as their own verses. They don't make eligible husbands! (aside to SERAPHINA).

Twin.

Confound their interruptions! (aside) My dear Madam, unless you pay the utmost attention you cannot catch the ideas. Are you ready ? Well, now you shall hear it to the end! (reads)— "Around my heart thou weavest a spell whose" —

Enter Zeke, L.

Zeke

Mister Augustus Fogg! A bery misty lookin young gemman? (aside)

Mrs. Tif.

Show him up, Adolph!

[Exit Zeke L.

Twin.

This is too much!

Sera.

Exquisite verses, Mr. Twinkle,—exquisite!

Twin.

Ah, lovely Seraphina! your smile of approval transports me to the summit of Olympus.

Sera.

Then I must frown, for I would not send you so far away.

Twin.

Enchantress! It's all over with her. (aside)

[Retire up and converse.

Mrs. Tif.

Mr. Fogg belongs to one of our oldest families,—to be sure he is the most difficult person in the world to entertain, for he never takes the trouble to talk, and never notices anything or anybody,—but then I hear that nothing is considered so vulgar as to betray any emotion, or to, attempt to render oneself agreeable!

Enter Mr. Fogg, L., fashionably attired but in very dark clothes.

Fogg.

(bowing stiffly) Mrs. Tiffany, your most obedient. Miss Seraphina, yours. How dye do Twinkle?

Mrs. Tif.

Mr. Fogg, how do you do? Fine weather,—delightful, isn't it?

Fogg.

I am indifferent to weather, Madam.

Mrs. Tif.

Been to the opera, Mr. Fogg? I hear that the bow monde make their debutt there every evening.

Fogg.

I consider operas a bore, Madam.

Sera.

(advancing) You must hear Mr. Twinkle's verses, Mr. Fogg!

Fogg.

I am indifferent to verses, Miss Serapbina.

Sera.

But Mr. Twinkle's verses are addressed to me!

Twin.

Now pay attention, Fogg! (reads)— "Around my heart thou weavest a spell

"Whose magic I"—

Enter Zeke L.

Zeke

Mister—No, he say he aint no Mister—

Twin.

"Around my heart thou weavest a spell whose magic I can never tell !"

Mrs. Tif.

Speak in a loud, clear tone, A-dolph!

Twin.

This is terrible!

Zeke

Mister Count Jolly-made-her!

Mrs. Tif.

Count Jolimaitre! Good gracious ! Zeke, Zeke—A-dolph I mean.— Dear me, what a mistake! (aside) Set that chair out of the way,—put that table back. Seraphina, my dear, are you all in order? Dear me! dear me! Your dress is so tumbled! (arranges her dress) What are you grinning at? (to ZEKE) Beg the Count to honor us by walking up!

[Exit Zeke, L.

Sera.

phina, my dear (aside to her), remember now what I told you about the Count. He is a man of the highest, good gracious! I am so flurried; and nothing is so ungenteel as agitation! what will the Count think! Mr. Twinkle, pray stand out of the way! Seraphina, my dear, place yourself on my right ! Mr. Fogg, the conservatory— beautiful flowers,—pray amuse yourself in the conservatory.

Fogg.

I am indifferent to flowers, Madam.

Fashion

Mrs. Tif.

Dear me! the man stands right in the way,—just where the Count must make his entray [aside. Mr. Fogg,—pray—

Enter Count Jolimaitre, L., very dashingly dressed, wears a moustache.

Mrs. Tif.

Oh, Count, this unexpected honor—

Sera.

Count, this inexpressible pleasure—

Count.

Beg you won't mention it, Madam! Miss Seraphina, your most devoted! (crosses to C.)

Mrs. Tif.

What condescension! (aside) Count may I take the liberty to introduce—Good gracious! I forgot. (aside) Count, I was about to remark that we never introduce in America. All our fashions are foreign, Count.

[Twinkle, who has stepped forward to be introduced, shows great indignation.

Count.

Excuse me, Madam, our fashions have grown antideluvian before you Americans discover their existence. You are lamentably behind the age—lamentably! 'Pon my honor, a foreigner of refinement finds great difficulty in existing in this provincial atmosphere.

Mrs. Tif.

How dreadful, Count! I am very much concerned. If there is anything which I can do, Count—

Sera.

R. Or I, Count, to render your situation less deplorable—

Count.

Ah! I find but one redeeming charm in America—the superlative loveliness of the feminine portion of creation,—and the wealth of their obliging papas. (aside)

Mrs. Tif.

How flattering! Ah! Count, I am afraid you will turn the head of my simple girl here. She is a perfect child of nature, Count.

Count.

Very possibly, for though you American women are quite charming, yet, demme, there's a deal of native rust to rub off!

Mrs. Tif.

Rust? Good gracious, Count! where do you find any rust? [looking about the room.

Count.

How very unsophisticated!

Mrs. Tif.

Count, I am so much ashamed,—pray excuse me! Although a lady of large fortune, and one, Count, who can boast of the highest connections, I blush to confess that I have never travelled,—while you, Count, I presume are at home in all the courts of Europe.

Count.

Courts ? Eh? Oh, yes, Madam, very true. I believe I am pretty well known in some of the courts of Europe—police courts. (aside, crossing, L.) In a word, Madam, I had seen enough of civilized life—wanted to refresh myself by a sight of barbarous countries and customs—had my choice between the Sandwich Islands and New York—chose New York!

Mrs. Tif.

How complimentary to our country! And, Count, I have no doubt you speak every conceivable language? You talk English like a native.

Count.

Eh, what? Like a native? Oh, ah, demme, yes, I am something of an Englishman. Passed one year and eight months with the Duke of Wellington, six months with Lord Brougham, two and a half with Count d'Orsay—knew them all more intimately than their best friends—no heroes to me—hadn't a secret from me, I assure you, especially of the toilet. (aside).

Mrs. Tif.

Think of that, my dear! Lord Wellington and Duke Broom! [aside to Seraphina.

Sera.

And only think of Count d'Orsay, Mamma! (aside to Mrs. Tiffany) I am so wild to see Count d'Orsay!

Count.

L. Oh ! a mere man milliner. Very little refinement out of Paris? Why at the very last dinner given at Lord—Lord Knows who, would you believe it, Madam, there was an individual present who wore a black cravat and took soup twice!

Mrs. Tif.

C. How shocking! the sight of him would have spoilt my appetite! Think what a great man he must be, my dear, to despise lords and counts in that way. (aside to Seraphina.) I must leave them together. (aside) Mr. Twinkle, your arm. I have some really very foreign exotics to show you.

Twin.

I fly at your command. I wish all her exotics were blooming in their native soil! [aside, and glancing at the Count.

Mrs. Tif.

Mr. Fogg, will you accompany us? My conservatory is well worthy a visit. It cost an immense sum of money.

Fogg.

I am indifferent to conservatories, Madam; flowers are such a bore!

Mrs. Tif.

I shall take no refusal. Conservatories are all the rage,—I could not exist without mine! Let me show you,—let me show you.

[places her arm through Mr. Fogg's, without his consent. Exeunt Mrs. Tiffany, Fogg, and Twinkle into the conservatory, where they are seen walking about.

Sera.

America, then, has no charms for you, Count?

Count.

Excuse me,—some exceptions. I find you, for instance, particularly charming! Can't say I admire your country. Ah! if you had ever breathed the exhilarating air of Paris, ate creams at Tortoni's, dined at the Café Royale, or if you had lived in London—felt at home at St.

James's, and every afternoon driven a couple of Lords and a Duchess through Hyde Park, you would find America—where you have no kings, queens, lords, nor ladies—insupportable!

Sera.

Not while there was a Count in it!

Enter Zeke, very indignant.

Zeke

Where's de Missus?

Enter Mrs. Tiffany, Fogg, and Twinkle, from the conservatory.

Mrs. Tif.

Whom do you come to announce, A-dolph?

Zeke

He said he wouldn't trust me—no, not eben wid so much as his name; so I wouldn't trust him up stairs, den he ups wid his stick and I cuts mine.

Mrs. Tif.

Some of Mr. Tiffany's vulgar acquaintances. I shall die with shame. (aside) A-dolph, inform him that I am not at home.

[Exit Zeke, L. U. E

My nerves are so shattered, I am ready to sink. Mr. Twinkle, that fow tool, if you please!

Twin.

What? What do you wish, Madam?

Mrs. Tif.

The ignorance of these Americans! (aside) Count, may I trouble you ? That fow tool, if you please—

Count.

She's not talking English, nor French, but I suppose it's American. (aside.)

True.

(outside) Not at home!

Zeke

No, Sar—Missus say she's not at home.

True.

Out of the way you grinning nigger!

Enter Adam Trueman, L. U. E., dressed as a farmer, a stout cane in his hand, his boots covered with dust. Zeke jumps out of his way as he enters.

[Exit Zeke, L.

True.

Where's this woman that's not at home in her own house? May I be shot! if I wonder at it! I shouldn't think she'd ever feel at home in such a show-box as this! (looking round.)

Mrs. Tif.

What a plebeian looking old farmer! I wonder who he is? (aside.) Sir—(advancing very agitatedly) what do you mean, Sir, by this owdacious conduct? How dare you intrude yourself into my parlor? Do you know who I am, Sir? (with great dignity) You are in the presence of Mrs. Tiffany, Sir!

True.

Antony's wife, eh? Well now, I might have guessed that—ha! ha! ha! for I see you make it a point to carry half your husband's shop upon your back! No matter; that's being a good helpmate—for he carried the whole of it once in a pack on his own shoulders—now you bear a share!

Mrs. Tif.

How dare you, you impertinent, owdacious, ignorant old man! It's all an invention. You're talking of somebody else. What will the Count think! (aside)

True.

Why, I thought folks had better manners in the city! This is a civil welcome for your husband's old friend, and after my coming all the way from Catterangus to see you and yours! First a grinning nigger tricked out in scarlet regimentals—

Mrs. Tif.

Let me tell you, Sir, that liveries are all the fashion!

True.

The fashion, are they? To make men wear the badge of servitude in a free land—that's the fashion, is it? Hurrah, for republican simplicity! I will venture to say now, that you have your coat of arms, too!

Mrs. Tif.

Certainly, Sir; you can see it on the panels of my voyture.

True.

Oh! no need of that. I know what your escutcheon must be! A bandbox rampant with a bonnet couchant, and a pedlar's pack passant! Ha, ha, ha! that shows both houses united!

25

Mrs. Tif.

Sir! you are most profoundly ignorant,—what do you mean by this insolence, Sir? How shall I get rid of him? (aside)

True.

(looking at Seraphina) I hope that is not Gertrude! (aside)

Mrs. Tif.

Sir, I'd have you know that—Seraphina, my child, walk with the gentlemen into the conservatory.

[Exeunt Seraphina, Twinkle, Fogg into conservatory.

Count Jolimaitre, pray make due allowances for the errors of this rustic! I do assure you, Count—(whispers to him)

True.

Count! She calls that critter with a shoe brush over his mouth, Count! To look at him, I should have thought he was a tailor's walking advertisement! (aside)

Count.

(addressing Trueman whom he has been inspecting through his eye-glass) Where did you say you belonged, my friend? Dug out of the ruins of Pompeii, eh?

True.

I belong to a land in which I rejoice to find that you are a foreigner.

Count.

What a barbarian! He doesn't see the honor I'm doing his country! Pray, Madam, is it one of the aboriginal inhabitants of the soil? To what tribe of Indians does he belong—the Pawnee or Choctaw? Does he carry a tomahawk?

True.

Something quite as useful,—do you see that?

[Shaking his stick. Count runs to R. H. behind Mrs. Tiffany.

Mrs. Tif.

Oh, dear! I shall faint! Millinette! (approaching R. D.) Millinette!

Enter Millinette, R. D., without advancing into the room.

Milli.

Oui, Madame.

Mrs. Tif.

A glass of water!

[Exit Millinette, r.

Sir, (Crossing L. to Trueman) I am shocked at your plebeian conduct! This is a gentleman of the highest standing, Sir! He is a Count, Sir!

Enter Millinette, R., bearing a salver with a glass of water. In advancing towards Mrs. TIFFANY, she passes in front of the Count, starts and screams. The Count, after a start of surprise, regains his composure, plays with his eye glass, and looks perfectly unconcerned.

Mrs. Tif.

What is the matter? What is the matter?

Milli.

Noting, noting,—only—(looks at Count and turns away her eyes again) only—noting at all!

True.

Don't be afraid, girl! Why, did you never see a live Count before? He's tame,—I dare say your mistress there leads him about by the ears.

Mrs. Tif.

This is too much! Millinette, send for Mr. Tiffany instantly!

[crosses to Millinette, who is going, 3 E. L.

Milli.

He just come in, Madame!

True.

My old friend! Where is he? Take me to him,—I long to have one more hearty shake of the hand!

Mrs. Tif.

Shake of the fist, you mean. (crosses to him) If I don't make him shake his in your face, you low, owdacious—no matter, we'll see! Count, honor me by joining my daughter in the conservatory, I will return immediately.

[Count bows and walks towards conservatory. Mrs. Tiffany following part of the way and then returning to Trueman.

True.

What a Jezebel! These women always play the very devil with a man, and yet I don't believe such a damaged bale of goods as that (looking at Mrs. Tiffany) has smothered the heart of little Antony!

Mrs. Tif.

This way, Sir, sal vous plait.

[Exit L. With great dignity.

True.

Sal vous plait. Ha, ha, ha! We'll see what Fashion has done for him.

[Exit L.

End of ACT I.

ACT II

SCENE I

Inner apartment of Mr. Tiffany's Counting House. Mr. Tiffany, R. c., seated at a desk looking over papers. Mr. Snobson, L. C., on a high stool at another desk, with a pen behind his ear.

Snobson.

(rising L., advances L. to the front of the stage, regards Tiffany and shrugs his shoulders) How the old boy frets and fames over those papers, to be sure! He's working himself into a perfect fever—exactly,—therefore bleeding's the prescription! So here goes! (aside) Mr. Tiffany, a word with you, if you please, Sir?

Tif.

(sitting still) Speak on, Mr. Snobson, I attend.

Snob.

What I have to say, Sir, is a matter of the first importance to the credit of the concern—the credit of the concern, Mr. Tiffany!

Tif.

Proceed, Mr. Snobson.

Snob.

Sir, you've a handsome house—fine carriage—nigger in livery—feed on the fat of the land—everything first rate—

Tif.

Well, Sir?

Snob.

My salary, Mr. Tiffany!

Tif.

It has been raised three times within the last year.

Snob.

Still it is insufficient for the necessities of an honest man,—mark me, an honest man, Mr. Tiffany.

Tif.

(crossing L.) What a weapon he has made of that word! (aside) Enough—another hundred shall be added. Does that content you?

Snob.

There is one other subject which I have before mentioned, Mr. Tiffany,—your daughter,—what's the reason you can't let the folks at home know at once that I'm to be the man?

Tif.

Villain! And must the only seal upon this scoundrel's lips be placed there by the hand of my daughter? (aside) Well, Sir, it shall be as you desire.

Snob.

And Mrs. Tiffany shall be informed of your resolution?

Tif.

Yes.

Snob.

Enough said! That's the ticket! The CREDIT of the concern's safe, Sir!

[returns to his seat.

Tif.

How low have I bowed to this insolent rascal! To rise himself he mounts upon my shoulders, and unless I can shake him off he must crush me! (aside)

Enter Trueman, C., down on L. H.

True.

Here I am, Antony, man! I told you I'd pay you a visit in your money-making quarters. (looks around) But it looks as dismal here as a cell in the States' Prison!

Tif.

(forcing a laugh) Ha, ha, ha ! States' Prison! You are so facetious! Ha, ha, ha!

True.

Well, for the life of me I can't see anything so amusing in that! I should think the States' Prison plaguy uncomfortable lodgings. And you laugh, man, as though you fancied yourself there already.

Tif.

Ha, ha, ha!

True.

(imitating him) Ha, ha, ha! What on earth do you mean by that ill-sounding laugh, that has nothing of a laugh about it! This fashion-worship has made heathens and hypocrites of you all! Deception is your household God! A man laughs as if he were crying, and cries as if he were laughing in his sleeve. Everything is something else from what it seems to be. I have lived in your house only three days, and I've heard more lies than were ever invented during a Presidential election! First your fine lady of a wife sends me word that she's not at home—I walk up stairs, and she takes good care that I shall not be at home—wants to turn me out of doors. Then you come in—take your old friend by the hand—whisper, the deuce knows what, in your wife's ear, and the tables are turned in a tangent! Madam curtsies—says she's enchanted to see me—and orders her grinning nigger to show me a room.

Tif.

We were exceedingly happy to welcome you as our guest!

True.

Happy? You happy? Ah! Antony! Antony! that hatchet face of yours, and those criss-cross furrows tell quite another story! It's many a long day since you were happy at anything! You look as if you'd melted down your flesh into dollars, and mortgaged your soul in the bargain! Your warm heart has grown cold over your ledger—your light spirits heavy with calculation! You have traded away your youth—your hopes—your tastes for wealth! and now you have the wealth you coveted, what does it profit you? Pleasure it cannot buy; for you have lost your capacity for enjoyment—Ease it will not bring; for the love of gain is never satisfied! It has made your counting-house a penitentiary, and your home a fashionable museum where there is no niche for you! You have spent so much time ciphering in the one, that you find yourself at last a very cipher in the other! See me, man! seventy-two last August!—strong as a hickory and every whit as sound!

Tif.

I take the greatest pleasure in remarking your superiority, Sir.

True.

Bah! no man takes pleasure in remarking the superiority of another! Why the deuce can't you speak the truth, man? But it's not the fashion I suppose! I have not seen one frank, open face since—no, no,

I can't say that either, though lying is catching! There's that girl, Gertrude, who is trying to teach your daughter music—but Gertrude was bred in the country!

Tif.

A good girl; my wife and daughter find her very useful.

True.

Useful? Well I must say you have queer notions of use!—But come, cheer up, man! I'd rather see one of your old smiles, than know you'd realized another thousand! I hear you are making money on the true, American, high pressure system—better go slow and sure—the more steam, the greater danger of the boiler's bursting! All sound, I hope? Nothing rotten at the core?

Tif.

Oh, sound—quite sound!

True.

Well that's pleasant—though I must say you don't look very pleasant about it!

Tif.

My good friend, although I am solvent, I may say, perfectly solvent—yet you—the fact is, you can be of some assistance to me!

True.

That's the fact is it? I'm glad we've hit upon one fact at last! Well—

[SNOBSON, who during this conversation has been employed in writing, but stops occasionally to listen, now gives vent to a dry chuckling laugh.

True.

Hey? What's that? Another of those deuced ill-sounding, city laughs! (sees Snobson) Who's that perched upon the stool of repentance—eh, Antony?

Snob.

The old boy has missed his text there—that's the stool of repentance!

[aside and looking at Tiffany's seat.

Tif.

One of my clerks—my confidential clerk!

True.

Confidential? Why he looks for all the world like a spy—the most inquisitorial, hang-dog face—ugh! the sight of it makes my blood run cold! Come, (crosses R.) let us talk over matters where this critter can't give us the benefit of his opinion! Antony, the next time you choose a confidential clerk, take one that carries his credentials in his face—those in his pocket are not worth much without!

[Exeunt Trueman and Tiffany, R. 1 E.

Snob.

(jumping from his stool and advancing C.) The old prig has got the tin, or Tiff would never be so civil! All right—Tiff will work every shiner into the concern—all the better for me! Now I'll go and make love to Seraphina. The old woman needn't try to knock me down with any of her French lingo! Six months from to-day if I ain't driving my two footmen tandem, down Broadway—and as fashionable as Mrs. Tiffany herself, then I ain't the trump I thought I was! that's all. (looks at his watch) Bless me! eleven o'clock and I haven't had my julep yet? Snobson, I'm ashamed of you!

[Exit, L.,

SCENE II

The interior of a beautiful conservatory; walk through the centre; stands of flower pots in bloom; a couple of rustic seats. Gertrude, R. C., attired in white, with a white rose in her hair; watering the flowers. Colonel Howard, L., regarding her.

How.

L. C. I am afraid you lead a sad life here, Miss Gertrude?

Ger.

R. C. (turning round gaily) What! amongst the flowers? (continues her occupation)

How.

No, amongst the thistles, with which Mrs. Tiffany surrounds you; the tempests, which her temper raises!

Ger.

They never harm me. Flowers and herbs are excellent tutors. I learn prudence from the reed, and bend until the storm has swept over me!

How.

Admirable philosophy! But still this frigid atmosphere of fashion must be uncongenial to you? Accustomed to the pleasant companionship of your kind friends in Geneva, surely you must regret this cold exchange?

Ger.

Do you think so? Can you suppose that I could possibly prefer a ramble in the woods to a promenade in Broadway? A wreath of scented wild flowers to a bouquet of these sickly exotics? The odour of new-mown hay to the heated air of this crowded conservatory? Or can you imagine that I could enjoy the quiet conversation of my

Geneva friends, more than the edifying chit-chat of a fashionable drawing room? But I see you think me totally destitute of taste?

How.

You have a merry spirit to jest thus at your grievances!

Ger.

I have my mania,—as some wise person declares that all mankind have,—and mine is a love of independence! In Geneva, my wants were supplied by two kind, old maiden ladies, upon whom I know not that I have any claim. I had abilities, and desired to use them. I came here at my own request; for here I am no longer dependent! Voila tout, as Mrs. Tiffany would say.

How.

Believe me, I appreciate the confidence you repose in me!

Ger.

Confidence! Truly, Colonel Howard, the confidence is entirely on your part, in supposing that I confide that which I have no reason to conceal! I think I informed you that Mrs. Tiffany only received visitors on her reception day—she is therefore not prepared to see you. Zeke—Oh! I beg his pardon—Adolph, made some mistake in admitting you.

How.

Nay, Gertrude, it was not Mrs. Tiffany, nor Miss Tiffany, whom I came to see; it—it was—

Ger.

The conservatory perhaps? I will leave you to examine the flowers at leisure! (crosses L.)

How.

Gertrude—listen to me. If I only dared to give utterance to what is hovering upon my lips! (aside) Gertrude!

Ger.

Colonel Howard!

How.

Gertrude, I must—must—

Ger.

Yes, indeed you must, must leave me! I think I hear somebody coming—Mrs. Tiffany would not be well pleased to find you here—pray, pray leave me—that door will lead you into the street.

[Hurries him out through door, C. F. ; takes up her watering pot, and commences watering flowers, tying up branches, &c.

What a strange being is man! Why should he hesitate to say—nay, why should I prevent his saying, what I would most delight to hear? Truly man is strange—but woman is quite as incomprehensible!

(walks about gathering flowers)

Enter Count Jolimaitre, L.

Count.

There she is—the bewitching little creature! Mrs. Tiffany and her daughter are out of ear-shot. I caught a glimpse of their feathers floating down Broadway, not ten minutes ago. Just the opportunity I have been looking for! Now for an engagement with this captivating little piece of prudery! 'Pon honor, I am almost afraid she will not resist a Count long enough to give value to the conquest. (approaches her) Ma belle petite, were you gathering roses for me?

Ger.

(starts on first perceiving him, but instantly regains her self-possession) The roses here, Sir, are carefully guarded with thorns—if you have the right to gather, pluck for yourself!

Count.

Sharp as ever, little Gertrude! But now that we are alone, throw off this frigidity, and be at your ease.

Ger.

Permit me to be alone, Sir, that I may be at my ease!

Count.

Very good, ma belle, well said! (applauding her with his hands) Never yield too soon, even to a title! But, as the old girl may find her way back before long, we may as well come to particulars at once. I love you; but that you know already. (rubbing his eye-glass unconcernedly with his handkerchief) Before long I shall make Mademoiselle Seraphina my wife, and, of course, you shall remain in the family!

Ger.

(indignantly) Sir—

Count.

'Pon my honor you shall!. In France we arrange these little matters without difficulty!

Ger.

But I am an American! Your conduct proves that you are not one!

[going, crosses, R. H.

Count.

(preventing her) Don't run away, my immaculate petite Americaine! Demme, you've quite overlooked my condescension—the difference of our stations—you a species of upper servant—an orphan—no friends.

Enter Trueman unperceived, R. U. E.

Ger.

And therefore more entitled to the respect and protection of every true gentleman! Had you been one, you would not have insulted me!

Count.

My charming little orator, patriotism and declamation become you particularly! (approaches her) I feel quite tempted to taste—

True.

(thrusting him aside) An American hickory switch! (strikes him) Well, how do you like it?

Count.

Old matter-of-fact! (aside) Sir, how dare you?

True.

My stick has answered that question!

Ger.

Oh! now I am quite safe!

True.

Safe! not a bit safer than before! All women would be safe, if they knew how virtue became them! As for you, Mr. Count, what have you to say for yourself? Come, speak out!

Count.

Sir,—aw—aw—you don't understand these matters.

True.

That's a fact! Not having had your experience, I don't believe I do understand them!

Count.

A piece of pleasantry—a mere joke—

True.

A joke was it? I'll show you a joke worth two of that! I'll teach you the way we natives joke with a puppy who don't respect an honest woman! (seizing him)

Count.

Oh! oh! demme—you old ruffian! let me go. What do you mean?

True.

Oh! a piece of pleasantry—a mere joke—very—pleasant isn't it?

[Attempts to strike him again; Count struggles with him. Enter Mrs. Tiffany hastily, L 2 E., in her bonnet and shawl.

Mrs. Tif.

What is the matter? I am perfectly abimé with terror. Mr. Trueman, what has happened?

True.

Oh! we have been joking!

Mrs. Tif.

(to Count, who is re-arranging his dress) My dear Count, I did not except to find you here—how kind of you!

True.

Your dear Count, has been showing his kindness in a very foreign manner. Too foreign I think, he found it to be relished by an unfashionable native! What do you think of a puppy, who insults an innocent girl all in the way of kindness? This Count of yours—this importation of—

Count.

My dear Madam, demme, permit me to explain. It would be unbecoming—demme—particularly unbecoming of you—aw—aw— to pay any attention to this ignorant person. (crosses to Trueman.) Anything that he says concerning a man of my standing—aw—the truth is, Madam—

True.

Let us have the truth by all means,—if it is only for the novelty's sake!

Count.

(turning his back to Trueman) You see, madam, hoping to obtain a few moments' private conversation with Miss Seraphina—with Miss Seraphina I say—and—aw—and knowing her passion for flowers, I found my way to your very tasteful and recherché conservatory. (looks about him approvingly) Very beautifully arranged—does you great credit, madam! Here I encountered this young person. She was inclined to be talkative; and I indulged her with—with a—aw— demme—a few common places! What passed between us was mere harmless badinage—on my part. You, madam, you—so conversant with our European manners—you are aware that when a man of fashion—that is, when a woman—a man is bound—amongst noblemen, you know—

Mrs. Tif.

I comprehend you perfectly—parfittement, my dear Count.

Count.

'Pon my honor, that's very obliging of her. (aside)

Mrs Tif.

I am shocked at the plebeian forwardness of this conceited girl!

True.

(walking up to Count) Did you ever keep a reckoning of the lies you tell in an hour?

Mrs Tif.

Mr. Trueman, I blush for you!

(crosses C., to Trueman)

True.

Don't do that—you have no blushes to spare!

Mrs. Tif.

It is a man of rank whom you are addressing, Sir!

True.

A rank villain, Mrs. Antony Tiffany! A rich one he would be, had he as much gold as brass!

Mrs. Tif.

Pray pardon him, Count; he knows nothing of how ton!

Count.

Demme, he's beneath my notice. I tell you what, old fellow— (Trueman raises his stick as Count approaches, the latter starts back) the sight of him discomposes me—aw—I feel quite uncomfortable— aw—let us join your charming daughter? I can't do you the honor to shoot you, Sir—(to Trueman) you are beneath me—a nobleman can't fight a commoner! Good bye, old Truepenny! I—aw—I'm insensible to your insolence!

[Exeunt Count and Mrs. Tiffany, R. H. U. E.

True.

You won't be insensible to a cow hide in spite of your nobility! The next time he practises any of his foreign fashions on you, Gertrude, you'll see how I'll wake up his sensibilities!

Ger.

I do not know what I should have done without you, sir.

True.

Yes, you do—you know that you would have done well enough! Never tell a lie, girl! not even for the sake of pleasing an old man! When you open your lips let your heart speak. Never tell a lie! Let your face be the looking-glass of your soul—your heart its clock— while your tongue rings the hours! But the glass must be clear, the clock true, and then there's no fear but the tongue will do its duty in a woman's head!

Ger.

You are very good, Sir!

True.

That's as it may be!—How my heart warms towards her! (aside) Gertrude, I hear that you have no mother?

Ger.

Ah! no, Sir; I wish I had.

True.

So do I! Heaven knows, so do I! (aside, and with emotion) And you have no father, Gertrude?

Ger.

No, Sir—I often wish I had!

True.

(hurriedly) Don't do that, girl! don't do that! Wish you had a mother—but never wish that you had a father again! Perhaps the one you had did not deserve such a child!

Enter Prudence, R. U. E., down L. H.

Pru.

Seraphina is looking for you, Gertrude.

Ger.

I will go to her. (crosses to R. H.) Mr. Trueman, you will not permit me to thank you, but you cannot prevent my gratitude! [Exit, R. U. E.

True.

(looking after her) If falsehood harbours there, I'll give up searching after truth!

[crosses R., retires up the stage musingly, and commences examining the flowers.

Pru.

What a nice old man he is to be sure! I wish he would say something! (aside)

[crosses R., walks after him, turning when he turns—after a pause,

Don't mind me, Mr. Trueman!

True.

Mind you? Oh! no, don't be afraid (crosses L.)—I wasn't minding you. Nobody seems to mind you much!

[continues walking and examining the flowers—Prudence follows.

Pru.

Very pretty flowers, ain't they? Gertrude takes care of them.

True.

Gertrude? So I hear—(advancing L. C.) I suppose you can tell me now who this Gertrude—

Pru.

Who she's in love with? I knew you were going to say that! I'll tell you all about it! Gertrude, she's in love with—Mr. Twinkle! and he's in love with her. And Seraphina she's in love with Count Jolly—what-d'ye-call-it: but Count Jolly don't take to her at all—but Colonel Howard—he's the man—he's desperate about her!

True.

Why you feminine newspaper! Howard in love with that quintessence of affectation! Howard—the only, frank, straightforward fellow that I've met since—I'll tell him my mind on the subject! And Gertrude hunting for happiness in a rhyming dictionary! The girl's a greater fool than I took her for! [crosses R.

Pru.

So she is—you see I know all about them!

True.

I see you do! You've a wonderful knowledge—wonderful—of other people's concerns! It may do here, but take my word for it, in the county of Catteraugus you'd get the name of a great busy-body. But perhaps you know that too?

Pru.

Oh! I always know what's coming. I feel it beforehand all over me. I knew something was going to happen the day you came here—and what's more I can always tell a married man from a single—I felt right off that you were a bachelor?

True.

Felt right off I was a bachelor did you? you were sure of it—sure?— quite sure? (Prudence assents delightedly) Then you felt wrong!—a bachelor and a widower are not the same thing!

Pru.

Oh! but it all comes to the same thing—a widower's as good as a bachelor any day! And besides I knew that you were a farmer right off.

True.

On the spot, eh? I suppose you saw cabbages and green peas growing out of my hat?

Pru.

No, I didn't—but I knew all about you. And I knew—(looking down and fidgetting with her apron) I knew you were for getting married soon! For last night I dream't I saw your funeral going along the streets, and the mourners all dressed in white. And a funeral is a sure sign of a wedding you know! (nudging him with her elbow)

True.

(imitating her voice). Well I can't say that I know any such thing! you know ! (nudging her back)

Pru.

Oh ! it does, and there's no getting over it! For my part, I like farmers—and I know all about setting hens and turkeys, and feeding chickens, and laying eggs, and all that sort of thing!

True.

May I be shot! if mistress newspaper is not putting in an advertisement for herself! This is your city mode of courting I suppose, ha, ha, ha! (aside)

Pru.

I've been west, a little; but I never was in the county of Catteraugus, myself.

True.

Oh. you were not? And you have taken a particular fancy to go there, eh?

Pru.

Perhaps I shouldn't object—

True.

Oh!—ah!—so I suppose. Now pay attention to what I am going to say, for it is a matter of great importance to yourself.

Pru.

Now it's coming—I know what he's going to say! (aside).

True.

The next time you want to tie a man for life to your apron-strings, pick out one that don't come from the county of Catteraugus—for green horns are scarce in those parts, and modest women plenty! [Exit, R.

Pru.

Now who'd have thought he was going to say that! But I won't give him up yet—I won't give him up. [Exit, R.

END OF ACT II.

ACT III

SCENE I

Mrs. Tiffany's Parlor. Enter Mrs. Tiffany, R. I E., followed by Mr. Tiffany.

Tif.

Your extravagance will ruin me, Mrs. Tiffany!

Mrs. Tif.

And your stinginess will ruin me, Mr. Tiffany! It is totally and toot a fate impossible to convince you of the necessity of keeping up appearances. There is a certain display which every woman of fashion is forced to make!

Tif.

And pray who made you a woman of fashion?

Mrs. Tif.

What a vulgar question! All women of fashion, Mr. Tiffany—

Tif.

In this land are self-constituted, like you, Madam—and fashion is the cloak for more sins than charity ever covered! It was for fashion's sake that you insisted upon my purchasing this expensive house—it was for fashion's sake that you ran me in debt at every exorbitant upholsterer's and extravagant furniture warehouse in the city—it was for fashion's sake that you built that ruinous conservatory— hired more servants than they have persons to wait upon—and dressed your footman like a harlequin!

Mrs. Tif.

Mr. Tiffany, you are thoroughly plebeian, and insufferably American, in your grovelling ideas! And, pray, what was the occasion of these very mal-ap-pro-pos remarks? Merely because I requested a paltry fifty dollars to purchase a new style of head-dress—a bijou of an article just introduced in France.

Tif.

Time was, Mrs. Tiffany, when you manufactured your own French head-dresses—took off their first gloss at the public balls, and then sold them to your shortest-sighted customers. And all you knew about France, or French either, was what you spelt out at the bottom of your fashion plates—but now you have grown so fashionable, forsooth, that you have forgotten how to speak your mother tongue!

Mrs. Tif.

Mr. Tiffany, Mr. Tiffany! Nothing is more positively vulgarian— more unaristocratic than any allusion to the past!

Tif.

Why I thought, my dear, that aristocrats lived principally upon the past—and traded in the market of fashion with the bones of their ancestors for capital?

Mrs. Tif.

Mr. Tiffany, such vulgar remarks are only suitable to the counting house, in my drawing room you should—

Tif.

Vary my sentiments with my locality, as you change your manners with your dress!

Mrs. Tif.

Mr. Tiffany, I desire that you will purchase Count d'Orsay's "Science of Etiquette," and learn how to conduct yourself—especially before you appear at the grand ball, which I shall give on Friday!

Tif.

Confound your balls, Madam; they make footballs of my money, while you dance away all that I am worth! A pretty time to give a ball when you know that I am on the very brink of bankruptcy!

Mrs. Tif.

So much the greater reason that nobody should suspect your circumstances, or you would lose your credit at once. Just at this crisis a ball is absolutely necessary to save your reputation! There is Mrs. Adolphus Dashaway—she gave the most splendid fjte of the season—and I hear on very good authority that her husband has not paid his baker's bill in three months. Then there was Mrs. Honeywood—

Tif.

Gave a ball the night before her husband shot himself—perhaps you wish to drive me to follow his example?

[crosses R. L. H.

Mrs. Tif.

Good gracious! Mr. Tiffany, how you talk! I beg you won't mention anything of the kind. I consider black the most unbecoming color. I'm sure I've done all that I could to gratify you. There is that vulgar old torment, Trueman, who gives one the lie fifty times a day—haven't I been very civil to him?

Tif.

Civil to his wealth, Mrs. Tiffany! I told you that he was a rich, old farmer—the early friend of my father my own benefactor—and that I had reason to think he might assist me in my present embarrassments. Your civility was bought—and like most of your own purchases has yet to be paid for.

[crosses to R. H.

Mrs. Tif.

And will be, no doubt! The condescension of a woman of fashion should command any price. Mr. Trueman is insupportably indecorous—he has insulted Count Jolimaitre in the most outrageous manner. If the Count was not so deeply interested—so abimi with Seraphina, I am sure he would never honor us by his visits again!

Tif.

So much the better—he shall never marry my daughter!—I am resolved on that. Why, Madam, I am told there is in Paris a regular matrimonial stock company, who fit out indigent dandies for this market. How do I know but this fellow is one of its creatures, and that he has come here to increase its dividends by marrying a fortune?

Mrs. Tif.

Nonsense, Mr. Tiffany. The Count, the most fashionable young man in all New York—the intimate friend of all the dukes and lords in Europe—not marry my daughter? Not permit Seraphina to become a Countess? Mr. Tiffany, you are out of your senses!

Tif.

That would not be very wonderful, considering how many years I have been united to you, my dear. Modern physicians pronounce lunacy infectious!

Mrs. Tif.

Mr. Tiffany, he is a man of fashion—

Tif.

Fashion makes fools, but cannot feed them. By the bye, I have a request,—since you are bent upon ruining me by this ball, and there is no help for it,—I desire that you will send an invitation to my confidential clerk, Mr. Snobson.

Mrs. Tif.

Mr. Snobson! Was there ever such an you-nick demand! Mr. Snobson would cut a pretty figure amongst my fashionable friends! I shall do no such thing, Mr. Tiffany.

Tif.

Then, Madam, the ball shall not take place. Have I not told you that I am in the power of this man? That there are circumstances which it is happy for you that you do not know—which you cannot comprehend,—but which render it essential that you should be civil to Mr. Snobson? Not you merely, but Seraphina also? He is a more appropriate match for her than your foreign favorite.

Mrs. Tif.

A match for Seraphina, indeed! (crosses) Mr. Tiffany, you are determined to make a fow pas.

Tif.

Mr. Snobson intends calling this morning.

[crosses to L. H.

Mrs Tif.

But, Mr. Tiffany, this is not reception day—my drawing-rooms are in the most terrible disorder—

Tif.

Mr. Snobson is not particular—he must be admitted.

Enter Zeke, L.

Zeke.

Mr. Snobson.

Enter Snobson, L.; exit Zeke, L.

Snob.

How dye do, Marm? (crosses to C.) How are you? Mr. Tiffany, your most!—

Mrs. Tif.

(formally) Bung jure. Comment vow porth, Monsur Snobson?

Snob.

Oh, to be sure—very good of you—fine day.

Mrs. Tif.

(pointing to a chair with great dignity) Sassoyez vow, Monsur Snobson.

Snob.

I wonder what she's driving at? I ain't up to the fashionable lingo yet! (aside) Eh? what? Speak a little louder, Marm?

Mrs. Tif.

What ignorance! (aside)

Tif.

I presume Mrs. Tiffany means that you are to take a seat.

Snob.

Ex-actly—very obliging of her—so I will. (sits) No ceremony amonst friends, you know—and likely to be nearer—you understand? O. K., all correct. How is Seraphina?

Mrs. Tif.

Miss Tiffany is not visible this morning. [retires up.

Snob.

Not visible? (jumping up, crosses, R.) I suppose that's the English for can't see her? Mr. Tiffany, Sir (walking up to him) what am I to understand by this de-fal-ca-tion, Sir? I expected your word to be as good as your bond—beg pardon, Sir—I mean better—considerably better—no humbug about it, Sir.

Tif.

Have patience, Mr. Snobson. (rings bell)

Enter Zeke, L.

Zeke, desire my daughter to come here.

Mrs. Tif.

(coming down, C.) Adolph—I say, Adolph—

[Zeke straightens himself and assumes foppish airs, as he turns to Mrs. Tiffany.

Tif.

Zeke.

Zeke.

Don't know any such nigga, Boss.

Tif.

Do as I bid you instantly, or off with your livery and quit the house!

Zeke.

Wheugh! I'se all dismission!

[exit, R.

Mrs. Tif.

A-dolph, A-dolph! (calling after him)

Snob.

I brought the old boy to his bearings, didn't I though! Pull that string, and he is sure to work right. (aside) Don't make any stranger of me, Marm—I'm quite at home. If you've got any odd jobs about the house to do up, I shan't miss you. I'll amuse myself with Seraphina when she comes—we'll get along very cosily by ourselves.

Mrs. Tif.

Permit we to inform you, Mr. Snobson, that a French mother never leaves her daughter alone with a young man—she knows your sex too well for that!

Snob.

Very dis-obliging of her—but as we're none French—

Mrs. Tif.

You have yet to learn, Mr. Snobson, that the American ee-light—the aristocracy—the how-ton—as a matter of conscience, scrupulously follow the foreign fashions.

Snob.

Not when they are foreign to their interests, Marm—for instance—
(enter Seraphina, R.) There you are at last, eh, Miss? How dye do!
Ma said you weren't visible. Managed to get a peep at her, eh, Mr.
Tiffany?

Sera.

I heard you were here, Mr. Snobson, and came without even
arranging my toilette; you will excuse my negligence?

Snob.

Of everything but me, Miss.

Sera.

I shall never have to ask your pardon for that, Mr. Snobson.

Mrs. Tif.

Seraphina—child—really—

[as she is approaching Seraphina, Mr. Tiffany plants himself in front
of his wife.

Tif.

Walk this way, Madam, if you please. To see that she fancies the
surly fellow takes a weight from my heart. (aside)

Mrs. Tif.

Mr. Tiffany, it is highly improper and not at all distingi to leave a
young girl—

[Enter Zeke, L.

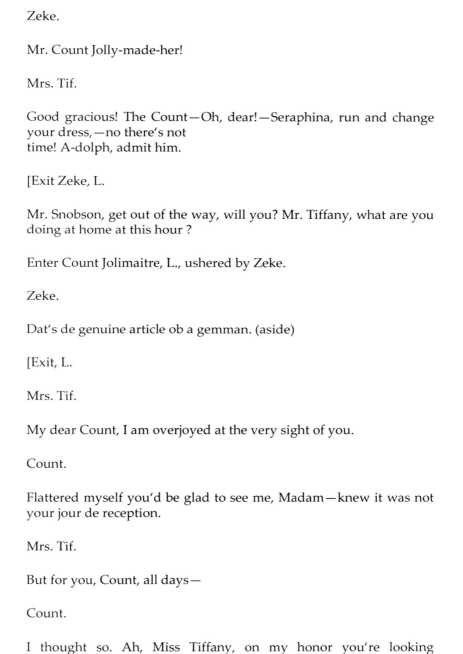

Zeke.

Mr. Count Jolly-made-her!

Mrs. Tif.

Good gracious! The Count—Oh, dear!—Seraphina, run and change your dress,—no there's not
time! A-dolph, admit him.

[Exit Zeke, L.

Mr. Snobson, get out of the way, will you? Mr. Tiffany, what are you doing at home at this hour ?

Enter Count Jolimaitre, L., ushered by Zeke.

Zeke.

Dat's de genuine article ob a gemman. (aside)

[Exit, L.

Mrs. Tif.

My dear Count, I am overjoyed at the very sight of you.

Count.

Flattered myself you'd be glad to see me, Madam—knew it was not your jour de reception.

Mrs. Tif.

But for you, Count, all days—

Count.

I thought so. Ah, Miss Tiffany, on my honor you're looking beautiful. [crosses R.

Sera.

Count, flattery from you—

Snob.

What? Eh? What's that you say?

Sera.

Nothing but what etiquette requires. [aside to him.

Count.

(regarding Mr. TIFFANY through his eye glass) Your worthy Papa, I believe? Sir, your most obedient.

[Mr. TIFFANY bows coldly; Count regards SNOBSON through his glass, shrugs his shoulders and turns away.

Snob.

(to Mrs. Tiffany) Introduce me, will you? I never knew a Count in all my life—what a strange-looking, animal!

Mrs. Tif.

Mr. Snobson, it is not the fashion to introduce in France!

Snob.

But, Marm, we're in America. (Mrs. T. crosses to Count, R.) The woman thinks she's somewhere else than where she is—she wants to make an alibi? (aside)

Mrs. Tif.

I hope that we shall have the pleasure of seeing you on Friday evening, Count?

Count.

Really, madam, my invitations—my engagements—so numerous—I can hardly answer for myself: and you Americans take offence so easily—

Mrs. Tif.

But, Count, everybody expects you at our ball—you are the principal attraction—

Sera.

Count, you must come!

Count.

Since you insist—aw—aw—there's no resisting you, Miss Tiffany.

Mrs. Tif.

I am so thankful. How can I repay your condescension! (Count and Seraphina converse) Mr Snobson, will you walk this way?—I have such a cactus in full bloom—remarkable flower! Mr. Tiffany, pray come here—I have something particular to say.

Tif.

Then speak out, my dear—I thought it was highly improper just now to leave a girl with a young man? [aside to her.

Mrs. Tif.

Oh, but the Count—that is different!

Tif.

I suppose you mean to say there's nothing of the man about him?

Enter Millinette, L., with a scarf in her hand.

Mil.

Adolph tell me he vas here. (aside) Pardon, Madame, I bring dis scarf for Mademoiselle.

Mrs. Tif.

Very well, Millinette; you know best what is proper for her to wear.

[Mr. and Mrs. Tiffany and Snobson retire up; she engages the attention of both gentlemen.

[Millinette crosses L., towards Seraphina, gives the Count a threatening look, and commences arranging the scarf over Seraphina's shoulders.

Mil.

Mademoiselle, permettez-moi. Perfide! (aside to Count) If Mademoiselle vil stand tranquille one petit moment. (turns Seraphina's back to the Count, and pretends to arrange the scarf) I must speak vid you to-day, or I tell all—you find me at de foot of de stair ven you go. Prend garde! (aside to Count)

Sera.

What is that you say, Millinette?

Mil.

Dis scarf make you so very beautiful, Mademoiselle—Je vous salue, mes dames. (curtsies) [exit, L.

Count.

Not a moment to lose! (aside) Miss Tiffany, I have an unpleasant—a particularly unpleasant piece of intelligence—you see, I have just received a letter from my friend—the—aw—the Earl of Airshire; the truth is, the Earl's daughter—beg you won't mention it—has distinguished me by a tender penchant.

Sera.

I understand—and they wish you to return and marry the young lady; but surely you will not leave, us, Count?

Count.

If you bid me stay—I shouldn't have the conscience—I couldn't afford to tear myself away. I'm sure that's honest (aside)

Sera.

Oh, Count!

Count.

Say but one word—say that you shouldn't mind being made a Countess—and I'll break with the Earl tomorrow.

Sera.

Count, this surprise—but don't think of leaving the country, Count—we could not pass the time without you! I—yes—yes, Count—I do consent!

Count.

I thought she would! (aside, while he embraces her) Enchanted, rapture, bliss, ecstacy, and all that sort of thing—words can't express it, but you understand. But it must be kept a secret—positively it must! If the rumour of our engagement were whispered abroad—the Earl's daughter—the delicacy, of my situation, aw—you comprehend? It is even possible that our nuptials, my charming Miss Tiffany, our nuptials must take place in private!

Sera.

Oh, that is quite impossible!

Count.

It's the latest fashion abroad—the very latest! Ah, I knew that would determine you. Can I depend on your secrecy?

Sera.

Oh, yes! Believe me.

Snob.

(coming forward in spite of Mrs. Tiffany's efforts to detain him) Why Seraphina, haven't you a word to throw to a dog?

Tif.

I shouldn't think she had after wasting so many upon a puppy. (aside)

Enter Zeke, L., wearing a three-cornered hat.

Zeke.

Missus, de bran new carriage am below.

Mrs. Tif.

Show it up,—I mean, Very well, A-dolph.

[Exit Zeke, L.

Count, my daughter and I are about to take an airing in our new voyture,—will you honor us with your company?

Count.

Madam, I—I have a most pressing engagement. A letter to write to the Earl of Airshire—who is at present residing in the Isle of Skye. I must bid you good morning.

Mrs. Tif.

Good morning, Count.

[Exit Count, L.

Snob.

I'm quite at leisure, (crosses to Mrs. T.) Marm. Books balanced—ledger closed—nothing to do all the afternoon,—I'm for you.

Mrs. Tif.

(without noticing him) Come, Seraphina, come! [as they are going Snobson follows them.

Snob.

But Marm—I was saying, Marm, I am quite at leisure—not a thing to do; have I, Mr. Tiffany?

Mrs. Tif.

Seraphina, child—your red shawl—remember— -Mr. Snobson, bon swear!

[Exit, L., leading Seraphina.

Snob.

Swear! Mr. Tiffany, Sir, am I to be fobbed off with a bon swear ? D-n it, I will swear!

Tif.

Have patience, Mr. Snobson, if you will accompany me to the counting house—

Snob.

Don't count too much on me, Sir. I'll make up no more accounts until these are settled! I'll run down and jump into the carriage in spite of her bon swear.

[Exit, L.

Tif.

You'll jump into a hornet's nest, if you do! Mr. Snobson, Mr. Snobson! [Exit after him.

[edit] SCENE II

Housekeeper's Room. Enter Millinette, R.

Mil.

I have set dat bjte, Adolph, to vatch for him. He say he would come back so soon as Madame's voiture drive from de door. If he not come—but he vill—he vill—he bien etourdi, but he have bon coeur.

Enter Count, L.

Count.

Ah! Millinette, my dear, you see what a good-natured dog I am to fly at your bidding—

Mil.

Fly? Ah! trompeur! Vat for you fly from Paris? Vat for you leave me—and I love you so much? Ven you sick—you almost die—did I not stay by you—take care of you—and you have no else friend ? Vat for you leave Paris?

Count.

Never allude to disagreeable subjects, mon enfant! I was forced by uncontrollable circumstances to fly to the land of liberty—

Mil.

Vat you do vid all de money I give you? The last sou I had—did I not give you?

Count.

I dare say you did, ma petite—wish you'd been better supplied! (aside) Don't ask any questions here—can't explain now—the next time we meet—

Mil.

But, ah! ven shall ve meet—ven? You not deceive me, not any more.

Count.

Deceive you! I'd rather deceive myself—I wish I could! I'd persuade myself you were once more washing linen in the Seine! (aside)

Mil.

I vil tell you ven ve shall meet—On Friday night Madame give one grand ball—you come sans doute—den ven de supper is served—de Americans tink of noting else ven de supper come—den you steal out of de room, and you find me here—and you give me one grand explanation!

Enter Gertrude, R., unperceived.

Count.

Friday night—while supper is serving—parole d'honneur I will be here—I will explain every thing—my sudden departure from Paris—my—demme, my countship—every thing! Now let me go—if any of the family should discover us—

Ger.

(who during the last speech has gradually advanced, L.) They might discover more than you think it advisable for them to know!

Count.

The devil!

Mil.

Mon Dieu! Mademoiselle Gertrude!

Count.

(recovering himself) My dear Miss Gertrude, let me explain—aw—aw—nothing is more natural than the situation in which you find me—

Ger.

I am inclined to believe that, Sir.

Count.

Now—'pon my honor, that's not fair. Here is Millinette will bear witness to what I am about to say—

Ger.

Oh, I have not the slightest doubt of that, Sir.

Count.

You see, Millinette happened to be lady's-maid in the family of—of—the Duchess Chateau D'Espague—and I chanced to be a particular friend of the Duchess—very particular I assure you! Of course I saw Millinette, and she, demme, she saw me! Didn't you, Millinette?

Mil.

Oh! oui—Mademoiselle I knew him ver vell.

Count.

Well, it is a remarkable fact that—being in correspondence with this very Duchess—at this very time—

Ger.

That is sufficient, Sir—I am already so well acquainted with your extraordinary talents for improvisation, that I will not further tax your invention—

Mil.

Ah! Mademoiselle Gertrude do not betray us—have pity!

Count.

(assuming an air of dignity) Silence, Millinette! My word has been doubted—the word of a nobleman! I will inform my friend, Mrs. Tiffany, of this young person's audacity. (going)

Ger.

His own weapons alone can foil this villain! (aside) Sir—Sir—Count! (at the last word the Count turns) Perhaps, Sir, the least said about this matter the better!

Count.

(delightedly) The least said? We won't say anything at all. She's coming round—couldn't resist me! (aside) Charming Gertrude—

Mil.

Quoi? Vat that you say?

Count.

My sweet, adorable Millinette, hold your tongue, will you? (aside to her)

Mil.

(aloud) No, I vill not! If you do look so from out your eyes at her again, I vill tell all!

Count.

Oh, I never could manage two women at once,—jealousy makes the dear creatures so spiteful. The only valor is in flight! (aside) Miss Gertrude, I wish you good morning. Millinette, mon enfant, adieu.

[Exit, L.

Mil.

But I have one word more to say. Stop, Stop!

[exit after him.

Ger.

(musingly) Friday night, while supper is serving, he is to meet Millinette here and explain—what? This man is an, impostor ? His insulting me—his familiarity with Millinette—his whole conduct— prove it. If I tell Mrs. Tiffany this she will disbelieve me, and one word may place this so-called Count on his guard. To convince Seraphina would be equally difficult, and her rashness and infatuation may render her miserable for life. No—she shall be saved! I must devise some plan for opening their eyes. Truly, if I cannot invent one, I shall be the first woman who was ever at a loss for a stratagem—especially to punish a villain or to shield a friend. [Exit, R.

End of ACT III.

ACT IV

SCENE I

Ball Room splendidly illuminated. A curtain hung at the further end. Mr. and Mrs. Tiffany, Seraphina, Gertrude, Fogg, Twinkle, Count, Snobson, Colonel Howard, a number of guests—some seated, some standing. As the curtain rises, a cotillion is danced; Gertrude dancing with Howard, Seraphina with Count.

Count.

(advancing with Seraphina to the front of the stage) To-morrow then—to-morrow—I may salute you as my bride—demme, my Countess!

Enter Zeke, L., with refreshments.

Sera.

Yes, to morrow.

[as the Count is about to reply, Snobson thrusts himself in front of Seraphina.

Snob.

You said you'd dance with me, Miss—now take my fin, and we'll walk about and see what's going on.

[Count raises his eye-glass, regards Snobson, and leads Seraphina away; Snobson follows, endeavoring to attract her attention, but encounters, on L. H., Zeke, bearing a waiter of refreshments; stops, helps himself, and puts some in his pockets.

Here's the treat! get my to-morrow's luncheon out of Tiff.

Enter Trueman, R, yawning and rubbing his eyes.

True.

What a nap I've had, to be sure! (looks at his watch) Eleven o'clock, as I'm alive! Just the time when country folks are comfortably turned in, and here your grand turn-out has hardly begun yet!

[to Tiffany, who approaches.

Ger.

(advancing R.) I was just coming to look for you, Mr. Trueman. I began to fancy that you were paying a visit to dream-land.

True.

So I was child—so I was—and I saw a face—like your's—but brighter!—even brighter. (to Tiffany) There's a smile for you, man! It makes one feel that the world has something worth living for in it yet! Do you remember a smile like that, Anthony? Ah! I see you don't—but I do—I do! (much moved)

How.

(advancing c.) Good evening, Mr. Trueman. [offers his hand.

True.

That's right man; give me your whole hand! When a man offers me the tips of his fingers, I know at once there's nothing in him worth seeking beyond his fingers ends.

[Trueman and Howard, Gertrude and Tiffany converse.

Mrs. Tif.

(advancing C.) I'm in such a fidget lest that vulgar old fellow should disgrace us by some of his plebeian remarks! What it is to give a ball, when one is forced to invite vulgar people!

[Mrs. Tiffany advances towards Trueman; Seraphina stands conversing flippantly with the gentlemen who surround her; amongst them is Twinkle, who having taken a magazine from his pocket, is reading to her, much to the undisguised annoyance of Snobson.

Dear me, Mr. Trueman, you are very late—quite in the fashion I declare!

True.

Fashion! And pray what is fashion, madam? An agreement between certain persons to live without using their souls! to substitute etiquette for virtue—decorum for purity—manners for morals! to affect a shame for the works of their Creator! and expend all their rapture upon the works of their tailors and dressmakers!

Mrs. Tif.

You have the most ow-tray ideas, Mr. Trueman—quite rustic, and deplorably American! But pray walk this way.

[Mrs. Tiffany and Trueman go up.

Count.

(advancing L., to Gertrude, who stands C., Howard R., a short distance behind her) Miss Gertrude—no opportunity of speaking to you before—in demand you know!

Ger.

I have no choice, I must be civil to him. (aside.) What were you remarking, Sir?

Count.

Miss Gertrude—charming Ger—aw—aw—I never found it so difficult to speak to a woman before. (aside)

Ger.

Yes, a very charming ball—many beautiful faces here.

Count.

Only one!—aw—aw—one—the fact is—[talks to her in dumb show, up C.

How.

What could old Trueman have meant by saying she fancied that puppy of a Count—that paste jewel thrust upon the little finger of society.

Count.

Miss Gertrude—aw—'pon my honor—you don't understand—really—aw—aw—will you dance the polka with me?

[Gertude bows and gives him her hand; he leads her to the set forming; Howard remains looking after them.

How.

Going to dance with him too! A few days ago she would hardly bow to him civilly—could old :Trueman
have had reasons for what he said? [retires up.

[Dance, the polka; Seraphina, after having distributed her bouquet, vinaigrette and fan amongst the gentlemen, dances with Snobson.

Pru.

(peeping in L., as dance concludes) I don't like dancing on Friday; something strange is always sure to happen! I'll be on the look out. [remains peeping and concealing herself when any of the company approach.

Ger.

(advancing hastily C.) They are preparing the supper—now if I can only dispose of Millinette while I unmask this insolent pretender! [Exit R.

Pru.

(peeping) What's that she said? It's coming!

Re-enter Gertrude, R., bearing a small basket filled with bouquets; approaches Mrs. Tiffany; they walk to the front of the stage.

Ger.

Excuse me, Madam—I believe this is just the hour at which you ordered supper?

Mrs. Tif.

Well, what's that to you! So you've been dancing with the Count—how dare you dance with a nobleman—you?

Ger.

I will answer that question half an hour hence. At present I have something to propose, which I think will gratify you and please your guests. I have heard that at the most elegant balls in Paris, it is customary—

Mrs. Tif.

What? what?

Ger.

To station a servant at the door with a basket of flowers. A bouquet is then presented to every lady as she passes in—I prepared this basket a short time ago. As the company walk in to supper, might not the flowers be distributed to advantage?

Mrs. Tif.

How distingui! You are a good creature, Gertrude—there, run and hand the bokettes to them yourself! You shall have the whole credit of the thing.

Ger.

Caught in my own net! (aside) But, madam, I know so little of fashions—Millinette, being French, herself will do it with so much more grace. I am sure Millinette—

Mrs. Tif.

So am I. She will do it a thousand times better than you—there go call her.

Ger.

(giving basket) But madam, pray order Millinette not to leave her station till supper is ended—as the company pass out of the supper room she may find that some of the ladies have been overlooked.

Mrs. Tif.

That is true—very thoughtful of you, Gertrude. [Exit Gertrude, R. What a recherchi idea!

Enter Millinette, R.

Here Millinette, take this basket. Place yourself there, (C.) and distribute these bokettes as the company pass in to supper; but remember not to stir from the spot until supper is over. It is a French fashion you know, Millinette. I am so delighted to be the first to introduce it—it will be all the rage in the bow-monde!

Mil.

Mon Dieu! dis vill ruin all! (aside) Madame, Madame, let me tell you, Madame, dat in France, in Paris, it is de custom to present les bouquets ven every body first come—long before de supper. Dis vould be outri! barbare! not at all la mode! Ven dey do come in dat is de fashion in Paris!

Mrs. Tif.

Dear me! Millinette what is the difference! besides I'd have you to know that Americans always improve upon French fashions! here, take the basket, and let me see that you do it in the most you-nick and genteel manner.

[Millinette poutingly takes the basket and retires up stage, L.a march. Curtain hung at the further end of the room is drawn back, and discloses a room, in the centre of which, stands a supper table, beautifully decorated and illuminated; the company promenade two by two into the supper room; Millinette presents bouquets as they pass; Count leads Mrs. Tiffany.

True.

(encountering Fogg, who is hurrying alone to the supper room) Mr. Fogg, never mind the supper, man! Ha, ha, ha! Of course you are indifferent to suppers!

Fogg.

Indifferent! suppers—oh ah—no Sir—suppers? no—no—I'm not indifferent to suppers! [hurries away towards table.

True.

Ha, ha, ha! Here's a new discovery I've made in the fashionable world! Fashion don't permit the critters to have heads or hearts, but it allows them stomachs! (to TIFFANY, who advances) So it's not fashionable to feel, but it's fashionable to feed, eh, Anthony? ha, ha, ha!

[Trueman and Tiffany retire towards supper room. Enter Gertrude, followed by Zeke, R.

Ger.

Zeke, go to the supper room instantly,—whisper to Count Jolimaitre that all is ready, and that he must keep his appointment without delay,—then watch him, and as he passes out of the room, place yourself in front of Millinette in such a manner, that the Count cannot see her nor she him. Be sure that they do not see each other—everything depends upon that. [crosses to R. H.

Zeke.

Missey, consider dat business brought to a scientific conclusion.

[Exit into supper room. Exit. Gertrude, R. H.

Pru.

(who has been listening) What can she want of the Count? I always suspected that Gertrude, because she is so merry and busy! Mr. Trueman thinks so much of her too—I'll tell him this! There's something wrong—but it all comes of giving a ball on a Friday! How astonished the dear old man will be when he finds out how much I know!

[advances timidly towards the supper room.

[edit] SCENE II

Housekeeper's room; dark stage; table, two chairs. Enter, Gertrude, with a lighted candle in her hand.

Ger.

So far the scheme prospers! and yet this imprudence—if I fail? Fail! to lack courage in a difficulty, or ingenuity in a dilemma, are not woman's failings!

Enter Zeke, R., with a napkin over his arm, and a bottle of champagne in his hand.

Well Zeke—Adolph!

Zeke.

Dat's right, Missey; I feels just now as if dat was my legitimate title; dis here's de stuff to make a nigger feel like a gemman!

Ger.

But is he coming?

Zeke.

He's coming! (sound of a champagne cork heard) Do you hear dat, Missey? Don't it put you all in a froth, and make you feel as light as a cork? Dere's nothing like the union brand, to wake up de harmonies ob de heart. [drinks from bottle.

Ger.

Remember to keep watch, upon the outside—do not stir from the spot; when I call you, come in quickly with a light—now, will you be gone!

Zeke.

I'm off, Missey, like a champagne cork wid de strings cut. [Exit R.

Ger.

I think I hear the Count's step, (crosses L., stage dark; she blows out candle) Now if I can but disguise my voice, and make the best of French.

Enter Count, R. H.

Count.

Millinette, where are you? How am I to see you in the dark?

Ger.

(imitating Millinette's voice in a whisper) Hush! parle bas.

Count.

Come here and give me a kiss.

Ger.

Non—non—(retreating alarmed, Count follows) make haste, I must know all.

Count.

You did not use to be so deuced particular.

Zeke.

(without) No admission, gemman! Box office closed, tickets stopped!

True.

(without) Out of my way; do you want me to try if your head is as hard as my stick?

Ger.

What shall I do? Ruined, ruined!

[she stands with her hand clasped in speechless despair.

Count.

Halloa! they are coming here, Millinette! Millinette, why don't you speak? Where can I hide myself? (running about stage, feeling for a door) Where are all your closets ? If I could only get out—or get in somewhere; may I be smothered in a clothes' basket, if you ever catch me in such a scrape again! (his hand accidentally touches the knob of a door opening into a closet, L. F.) Fortune's favorite yet! I'm safe!

[gets into closet and closes door. Enter Prudence, Trueman, Mrs. Tiffany, and Colonel Howard, R., followed by Zeke, bearing a light; lights up.

Pru.

Here they are, the Count and Gertrude! I told you so! [stops in surprise on seeing only Gertrude.

True.

And you see what a lie you told!

Mrs. Tif.

Prudence, how dare you create this disturbance in my house? To suspect the Count too—a nobleman!

How.

My sweet Gertrude, this foolish old woman would—

Pru.

Oh! you needn't talk—I heard her make the appointment—I know he's here—or he's been here. I wonder if she hasn't hid him away! [runs peeping about the room.

True.

(following her angrily) You're what I call a confounded—troublesome—meddling—old—prying—(as he says the last word, PRUDENCE opens closet where the Count is concealed) Thunder and lightning!

Pru.

I told you so!

[they all stand aghast; Mrs. Tiffany, R., with her hands lifted in surprise and anger; Trueman, R. C., clutching his stick; Howard, L. C., looking with an expression of bewildered horror from the Count to Gertrude.

Mrs.. Tif. (shaking her fist at Gertrude) You depraved little minx! this is the meaning of your dancing with the Count!

Count.

(stepping from the closet and advancing L. H.) I don't know what to make of it! Millinette not here! Miss Gertrude—oh! I see—a disguise—the girl's desperate about me—the way with them all. (aside)

True.

I'm choking—I can't speak—Gertrude—no—no —it is some horrid mistake! (partly aside, changes his tone suddenly) The villain! I'll hunt the truth out of him, if there's any in—(crosses L., approaches Count threateningly) do you see this stick? You made its first acquaintance a few days ago; it is time you were better known to each other.

[as Trueman attempts to seize him, Count escapes, crosses R., and shields himself behind Mrs. Tiffany, Trueman following.

Count.

You ruffian! would you strike a woman?—Madam—my dear Madam—keep off that barbarous old man, and I will explain! Madam, with—aw—your natural bon gout—aw—your fashionable refinement—aw—your—aw—your knowledge of foreign customs—

Mrs. Tif.

Oh! Count, I hope it ain't a foreign custom for the nobility to shut themselves up in the dark with young women? We think such things dreadful in America.

Count.

Demme—aw—hear what I have to say, Madam—I'll satisfy all sides—I am perfectly innocent in this affair —'pon my honor I am! That young lady shall inform you that I am so herself!—can't help it, sorry for her. Old matter-of-fact won't be convinced any other way,—that club of his is so particularly unpleasant! (aside) Madam, I was summoned here malgri moi, and not knowing whom, I was to meet—Miss Gertrude, favor this company by saying whether or not you directed—that—aw—aw—that colored individual to conduct me here?

Ger.

Sir, you well know-

Count.

A simple yes or no will suffice.

Mrs. Tif.

Answer the Count's question instantly, Miss.

Ger.

I did—but—

Count.

You hear, Madam—

True.

I won't believe it—I cant! Here you nigger, stop rolling up your eyes, and let us know whether she told you to bring that critter here?

Zeke.

I'se refuse to gib ebidence; dat's de device ob de skilfullest counsels ob de day! Can't answer, Boss—neber git a word out ob dis child— Yah! yah! [Exit.

Ger.

Mrs. Tiffany,—Mr. Trueman, if you will but have patience—

True.

Patience! Oh, Gertrude, you've taken from an old man something better and dearer than his patience—the one bright hope of nineteen years of self-denial—of nineteen years of—

[throws himself upon a chair, his head leaning on table.

Mrs. Tif.

Get out of my house, you owdacious—you ruined—you abimi young woman! You will corrupt all my family. Good gracious! don't touch me,—don't come near me. Never let me see your face after to-morrow. Pack.

[goes up

How.

Gertrude, I have striven to find some excuse for you—to doubt—to disbelieve—but this is beyond all endurance! [Exit, R. H.

Enter Millinette in haste, R.

Mil.

I could not come before—(stops in surprise at seeing the persons assembled) Mon Dieu! vat does dis mean?

Count.

Hold your tongue, fool! You will ruin everything, I will explain to-morrow. (aside to her) Mrs. Tiffany—Madam—my dear Madam, let me conduct you back to the ball-room. (she takes his arm) You see I am quite innocent in this matter; a man of my standing, you know,—aw, aw—you comprehend the whole affair.

[Exit Count leading Mrs. T., R. H.

Mil.

I vill say to him von vord, I will! [Exit, R.

Ger.

Mr. Trueman, I beseech you—I insist upon being heard,—I claim it as a right!

True.

Right? How dare you have the face, girl, to talk of rights? (comes down) You had more rights than you thought for, but you have forfeited them all! All right to love, respect, protection, and to not a little else that you don't dream of. Go, go! I'll start for Catteraugus to-morrow,—I've seen enough of what fashion can

do! [Exit, R. H.

Pru.

(Wiping her eyes) Dear old man, how he takes on! I'll go and console him! [Exit, R. H.

Ger.

This is too much! How heavy a penalty has my imprudence cost me!—his esteem, and that of one dearer—my home—my—(burst of lively music from ball-room) They are dancing, and I—I should be weeping, if pride had not sealed up my tears.

[She sinks into a chair. Band plays the polka behind till Curtain falls.

End of ACT IV.

ACT V

SCENE I

Mrs. Tiffany's Drawing Room—same Scene as Act 1st. Getrude seated, R. at a table, with her head leaning on her hand; in the other hand she holds a pen. A sheet of paper and an inkstand before her.

Ger.

How shall I write to them? What shall I say? Prevaricate I cannot—(rises and comes forward) and yet if I write the truth—simple souls! how can they comprehend the motives for my conduct? Nay—the truly pure see no imaginary—evil in others! It is only vice, that reflecting its own image, suspects even the innocent. I have no time to lose—I must prepare them for my return, (resumes her seat and writes) What a true pleasure there is in daring to be frank! (after writing a few lines more pauses) Not so frank either,—there is one name that I cannot mention. Ah! that he should suspect—should despise me. (writes)

Enter Trueman, L.

True.

There she is! If this girl's soul had only been as fair as her face,—yet she dared to speak the truth,—I'll not forget that! A woman who refuses to tell a lie has one spark of heaven in her still. (approaches her) Gertrude,

[Gertrude starts and looks up.

What are you writing there ? Plotting more mischief, eh, girl?

Ger.

I was writing a few lines to some friends in Geneva.

86

Fashion

True.

The Wilsons, eh?

Ger.

(surprised, rising) Are you acquainted with them, Sir?

True.

I shouldn't wonder if I was. I suppose you have taken good care not to mention the dark room—that foreign puppy in the closet—the pleasant surprise—and all that sort of thing, eh?

Ger.

I have no reason for concealment, Sir! for I have done nothing of which I am ashamed!

True.

Then I can't say much for your modesty.

Ger.

I shouldn't wish you to say more than I deserve.

True.

There's a bold minx! (aside)

Ger.

Since my affairs seem to have excited your interest—I will not say curiosity, perhaps you even feel a desire to inspect my correspondence? There, (handing the letter) I pride myself upon my good nature,—you may like to take advantage of it?

True.

With what an air she carries it off! (aside) Take advantage of it? So I will. (reads) What's this? "French chambermaid — Count—impostor—infatuation—Seraphina—Millinette—disguised myself—expose him." Thunder and lightning! I see it all! Come and kiss me, girl! (Gertrude evinces surprise) No, no—I forgot—it won't do to come to that yet! She's a rare girl! I'm out of my senses with joy! I don't know what to do with myself! Tol, de rol, de rol, de ra! [capers and sings.

Ger.

What a remarkable old man! (aside) Then you do me justice, Mr. Trueman?

True.

I say I don't! Justice? You're above all dependence upon justice! Hurrah! I've found one true woman at last? True? (pauses thoughtfully) Humph! I didn't think of that flaw! Plotting and manoeuvering—not much truth in that? An honest girl should be above stratagems!

Ger.

But my motive, Sir, was good.

True.

That's not enough—your actions must be good as well as your motives! Why could you not tell the silly girl that the man was an impostor?

Ger.

I did inform her of my suspicions—she ridiculed them; the plan I chose was an imprudent one, but I could not devise—

True.

I hate devising! Give me a woman with the firmness to be frank! But no matter—I had no right to look for an angel out of Paradise; and I am as happy—as happy as a Lord! that is, ten times happier than any Lord ever was! Tol, de rol, de rol! Oh! you—you—I'll thrash every fellow that says a word against you!

Ger.

You will have plenty of employment then, Sir, for I do not know of one just now who would speak in my favor!

True.

Not one, eh? Why, where's your dear Mr. Twinkle? I know all about it—can't say that I admire your choice of a husband! But there's no accounting for a girl's taste.

Ger.

Mr. Twinkle! Indeed you are quite mistaken!

True.

No—really? Then you're not taken with him, eh?

Ger.

Not even with his rhymes.

True.

Hang that old mother meddle-much! What a fool she has made of me. And so you're quite free, and I may choose a husband for you myself? Heart-whole, eh?

Ger.

I—I—I trust there is—nothing unsound about my heart.

True.

There it is again. Don't prevaricate, girl! I tell you an evasion is a lie in contemplation, and I hate lying! Out with the truth! Is your heart free or not?

Ger.

Nay, Sir, since you demand an answer, permit me to demand by what right you ask the question?

Enter Howard, L.

Colonel Howard here!

True.

I'm out again! What's the Colonel to her?

[retires up

How.

(crosses to her) I have come, Gertrude, to bid you farewell. To-morrow I resign my I commission and leave this city, perhaps for ever. You, Gertrude, it is you who have exiled me! After last evening—

True.

(coming forward C. Howard) What the plague have you got to say about last evening?

How.

Mr. Trueman!

True.

What have you got to say about last evening? and what have you to say to that little girl at all? It's Tiffany's precious daughter that you're in love with.

How.

Miss Tiffany? Never! I never had the slightest pretension —

True.

That lying old woman! But I'm glad of it! Oh! Ah! Um! (looking significantly at Gertrude and then at Howard) I see how it is. So you don't choose to marry Seraphina, eh? Well now, whom do you choose to marry? [glancing at Gertrude.

How.

I shall not marry at all!

True.

You won't? (looking at them both again) Why you don't mean to say that you don't like — [points with his thumb to Gertrude.

Ger.

Mr. Trueman, I may have been wrong to boast of my good nature, but do not presume too far upon it.

How.

You like frankness, Mr. Trueman, therefore I will speak plainly. I have long cherished a dream from which I was last night rudely awakened.

True.

And that's what you call speaking plainly? Well, I differ with you! But I can guess what you mean. Last night you suspected Gertrude there of—(angrily) of what no man shall ever suspect her again while I'm above ground! You did her injustice,—it was a mistake! There, now that matter's settled. Go, and ask her to forgive you,—-she's woman enough to do it! Go, go!

How.

Mr. Trueman, you have forgotten to whom you dictate.

True.

Then you won't do it? you wont ask her pardon?

How.

Most undoubtedly I will not—not at any man's bidding. I must first, know—

True.

You wont do it? Then if I don't give you a lesson in politeness—

How.

It will be because you find me your tutor in the same science. I am not a man to brook an insult, Mr. Trueman! but we'll not quarrel in presence of the lady.

True.

Won't we? I don't know that—

[crosses R. H.

Ger.

Pray, Mr. Trueman—Colonel Howard, (crosses to C,.) pray desist, Mr. Trueman, for my sake! (taking hold of his arm to hold him back) Colonel Howard, if you will read this letter it will explain everything.

[hands letter to Howard, who reads.

True.

He don't deserve an explanation! Didn't I tell him that it was a mistake? Refuse to beg your pardon! I'll teach him, I'll teach him!

How.

(after reading) Gertrude, how have I wronged you!

True.

Oh, you'll beg her pardon now? [between them.

How.

Her's, Sir, and your's! Gertrude, I fear—

True.

You needn't—she'll forgive you. You don't know these women as well as I do,—they're always ready to pardon; it's their nature, and they cant help it. Come along, I left Antony and his wife in the dining room; we'll go and find them. I've a story of my own to tell! As for you, Colonel, you may follow. Come along, Come along!

[Leads out Gertrude, R., followed by Howard.

Enter Mr. and Mrs. Tiffany, L. U. E. Mr. Tiffany with a bundle of bills in his hand.

Mrs. Tif.

I beg you won't mention the subject again, Mr. Tiffany. Nothing is more plebeian than a discussion upon economy—nothing more ungenteel than looking over and fretting over one's bills!

Tif.

Then I suppose, my dear, it is quite as ungenteel to pay one's bills?

Mrs. Tif.

Certainly! I hear the ee-light never condescend to do anything of the kind. The honor of their invaluable patronage is sufficient, for the persons they employ!

Tif.

Patronage then is a newly invented food upon which the working classes fatten? What convenient appetites poor people must have! Now listen, to what I am going to say. As soon as my daughter marries Mr. Snobson—

Enter Prudence, R., a three-cornered note in her hand.

Pru.

Oh, dear! oh, dear! what shall we do! Such a misfortune! Such a disaster! Oh, dear! oh, dear!

Mrs. Tif.

Prudence, you are the most tiresome creature! What is the matter?

Pru.

(pacing up and down the stage) Such a disgrace to the whole family! But I always expected it. Oh, dear! oh, dear!

Mrs. Tif.

(following her up and down the stage) What are you talking about, Prudence? Will, you tell me what has happened?

Pru.

(still pacing, Mrs. Tiffany following) Oh! I can't I can't! You'll feel so dreadfully! How could she do such a thing! But I expected nothing else! I never did, I never did!

Mrs. Tif.

(still following) Good gracious! what do you mean, Prudence? Tell me, will you tell me? I shall get into such a passion! What is the matter?

Pru.

(still pacing) Oh, Betsy, Betsy! That your daughter should have come to that! Dear me, dear me!

Tif.

Seraphina? Did you say Seraphina? What has happened to her? what has she done?

[following Prudence up and down the stage on the opposite side from Mrs. Tiffany.

Mrs. Tif.

(still following) What has she done? what has she done?

Pru.

Oh something dreadful—dreadful—shocking!

Tif.

(still following) Speak quickly and plainly—you torture me by this delay,—Prudence, be calm, and speak! What is it?

Pru.

(stopping) Zeke just told me—he carried her travelling trunk himself—she gave him a whole dollar! Oh, my!

Tif.

Her trunk? where? where?

Pru.

Round the corner!

Mrs. Tif.

What did she want with her trunk? You are the most vexatious creature, Prudence! There is no bearing your ridiculous conduct!

Pru.

Oh, you will have worse to bear—worse! Seraphina's gone!

Tif.

Gone! where?

Pru.

Off!—eloped—eloped with the Count! Dear me, dear me! I always told you she would!

Tif.

Then I am ruined!

[stands with his face buried in his hands.

Mrs. Tif.

Oh, what a ridiculous girl! And she might have had such a splendid wedding! What could have possessed her?

Tif.

The devil himself possessed her, for she has ruined me past all redemption! Gone, Prudence, did you say gone? Are you sure they are gone?

Pru.

Didn't I tell you so! Just look at this note—one might know by the very fold of it—

Tif.

(snatching the note) Let me see it! (opens the note and reads)
"My dear Ma,—When you receive this I shall be a countess! Isn't it a sweet title? The Count and I were forced to be married privately, for reasons which I will explain in my next. You must pacify Pa, and put him in a good humour before I come back, though now I'm to be a countess I suppose I shouldn't care!" Undutiful huzzy! "We are going to make a little excursion and will be back in a week—Your dutiful daughter—Seraphina."
A man's curse is sure to spring up at his own hearth,—here is mine! The sole curb upon that villain gone, I am wholly in his power! Oh! the first downward step from honor—he who takes it cannot pause in his mad descent, and is sure to be hurried on to ruin!

Mrs. Tif.

Why, Mr. Tiffany, how you do take on! And I dare say to elope was the most fashionable way after all!

Enter Trueman, R., leading Gertrude, and followed by Howard.

True.

Where are all the folks? Here, Antony—you are the man I want. We've been hunting for you all over the house. Why—what's the matter? There's a face for a thriving city merchant! Ah! Antony, you never wore such a hang-dog look as that when you trotted about the country with your pack upon your back! Your shoulders are no broader now—but they've a heavier load to carry—that's plain!

Mrs. Tif.

Mr. Trueman, such allusions are highly improper! What would my daughter, the Countess, say!

Ger.

The Countess? Oh! Madam!

Mrs. Tif.

Yes, the Countess! My daughter Seraphina, the Countess dee Jolimaitre! What have you to say to that? No wonder you are surprised after your recherchi abimi conduct! I have told you already, Miss Gertrude, that you were not a proper person to enjoy the inestimable advantages of my patronage. You are dismissed—do you understand? Discharged!

True.

Have you done? Very well, it's my turn now. Antony, perhaps what I have to say don't concern you as much as some others—but I want you to listen to me. You remember, Antony, (his tone becomes serious), a blue-eyed, smiling girl—

Tif.

Your daughter, Sir? I remember her well.

True.

None ever saw her to forget her! Give me your hand, man. There—that will do! Now let me go on. I never coveted wealth—yet twenty years ago I found myself the richest farmer in Catteraugus. This cursed money made my girl an object of speculation. Every idle fellow that wanted to feather his nest was sure to come courting Ruth. There was one—my heart misgave me the instant I laid eyes upon him—for he was a city chap, and not over fond of the truth. But Ruth—ah! she was too pure herself to look for guile! His fine words and his fair looks—the old story—she was taken with him—I said, "no"—but the girl liked her own way better than her old father's—girls always do! and one morning—the rascal robbed me—not of my money, he would have been welcome to that—but of the only treasure I cherished—my daughter!

Tif.

But you forgave her!

True.

I did! I knew she would never forgive herself—that was punishment enough! The scoundrel thought he was marrying my gold with my daughter—he was mistaken! I took care that they should never want; but that was all. She loved him—what will not woman love? The villain broke her heart—mine was tougher, or it wouldn't have stood what it did. A year after they were married,—he forsook her! She came back to her old home—her old father! It couldn't last long—she pined—and pined—and—then—she died! Don't think me an old fool—though I am one—for grieving won't bring her back. (bursts into tears.)

Tif.

It was a heavy loss!

True.

So heavy, that I should not have cared how soon I followed her, but for the child she left! As I pressed that child in my arms, I swore that my unlucky wealth should never curse it, as it had cursed its mother!

It was all I had to love—but I sent it away—and the neighbors thought it was dead. The girl was brought up tenderly but humbly by my wife's relatives in Geneva. I had her taught true independence—she had hands—capacities—and should use them! Money should never buy her a husband! for I resolved not to claim her until she had made her choice, and found the man who was willing to take her for herself alone. She turned out a rare girl! and it's time her old grandfather claimed her. Here he is to do it! And there stands Ruth's child! Old Adam's heiress! Gertrude, Gertrude!—my child!

[Gertrude rushes into his arms.

Pru.

(After a pause) Do tell; I want to know! But I knew it! I always said Gertrude would turn out somebody, after all!

Mrs. Tif.

Dear me! Gertrude an heiress! My dear Gertrude, I always thought you a very charming girl—quite you-nick—an heiress! I must give her a ball! I'll introduce her into society myself—of course an heiress must make a sensation! (aside)

How.

I am too bewildered even to wish her joy. Ah! there will be plenty to do that now—but the gulf between us is wider than ever. (aside)

True.

Step forward, young man, and let us know what you are muttering about. I said I would never claim her until she had found the man who loved her for herself. I have claimed her—yet I never break my word—I think I have found that man! and here he is. (strikes Howard on the shoulder) Gertrude's your's! There—never say a word, man—don't bore me with your thanks—you can cancel all obligations by making that child happy! There—take her!—Well, girl, and what do you say?

Ger.

That I rejoice too much at having found a parent for my first act to be one of disobedience!

[gives her hand to Howard.

True.

How very dutiful! and how disinterested!

[Tiffany retires up—and paces the stage, exhibiting great agitation.

Pru.

(to Trueman) All the single folks are getting married!

True.

No they are not. You and I are single folks, and we're not likely to get married.

Mrs. Tif.

My dear Mr. Trueman—my sweet Gertrude, when my daughter, the Countess, returns, she will be delighted to hear of this deenooment! I assure you that the Countess will be quite charmed!

Ger.

The Countess? Pray Madam where is Seraphina?

Mrs. Tif.

The Countess dee Jolimaitre, my dear, is at this moment on her way to—to Washington! Where after visiting all the fashionable curiosities of the day—including the President—she will return to grace her native city!

Ger.

I hope you are only jesting, Madam? Seraphina is not married?

Mrs. Tif.

Excuse me, my dear, my daughter had this morning the honor of being united to the Count dee Jolimaitre!

Ger.

Madam! He is an impostor!

Mrs. Tif.

Good gracious! Gertrude, how can you talk in that disrespectful way of a man of rank? An heiress, my dear, should have better manners! The Count—

Enter Millinette, R., crying.

Mil.

Oh! Madame! I will tell everyting—oh! dat monstre. He break my heart!

Mrs. Tif.

Millinette, what is the matter?

Mil.

Oh! he promise to marry me—I love him much—and now Zeke say he run away vid Mademoiselle Seraphina!

Mrs. Tif.

What insolence! The girl is mad! Count Jolimaitre marry my femmy de chamber!

Mil.

Oh! Madame, he is not one Count, not at all! Dat is only de title he go by in dis country. De foreigners always take de large title ven dey do come here. His name ` Paris vas Gustave Tread-mill. But he not one Frenchman at all, but he do live one long time ` Paris. First he live vid Monsieur Vermicelle—dere he vas de head cook! Den he live vid Monsieur Tire-nez, de barber! After dat he live vid Monsieur le Comte Frippon-fin—and dere he vas le Comte's valet! Dere, now I tell everyting I feel one great deal better!

Mrs. Tif.

Oh! good gracious! I shall faint! Not a Count! What will every body say? It's no such thing! I say he is a Count! One can see the foreign jenny says quoi in his face! Don't you think I can tell a Count when I see one? I say he is a Count!

Enter Snobson, L., his hat on—his hands thrust in his pocket— evidently a little intoxicated.

Snob.

I won't stand it! I say I won't!

Tif.

(rushing up to him) Mr. Snobson, for heaven's sake— (aside)

Snob.

Keep off! I'm a hard customer to get the better of! You'll see if I don't come out strong!

True.

(quietly knocking off Snobson's hat with his stick) Where are your manners, man?

Snob.

My business ain't with you, Catteraugus; you've waked up the wrong passenger!—Now the way I'll put it into Tiff will be a caution. I'll make him wince! That extra mint julep has put the true pluck in me. Now for it! (aside) Mr. Tiffany, Sir—you needn't think to come over me, Sir—you'll have to get up a little earlier in the morning before you do that, Sir! I'd like to know, Sir, how you came to assist your daughter in running away with that foreign-loafer? It was a downright swindle, Sir. After the conversation I and you had on that subject she wasn't your property, Sir.

True.

What, Antony is that the way your city clerk bullies his boss?

Snob.

You're drunk, Catteraugus—don't expose yourself—you're drunk! Taken a little too much toddy, my old boy! Be quiet! I'll look after you, and they won't find it out. If you want to be busy, you may take care of my hat—I feel so deuced weak in the chest; I don't think I could pick it up myself.—Now to put the screws to Tiff. (aside) Mr. Tiffany, Sir—you have broken your word, as no virtuous individual—no honorable member—of—the com—mu—ni—ty—

Tif.

Have some pity, Mr. Snobson, I beseech you! I had nothing to do with my daughter's elopement! I will agree to anything you desire— your salary shall be doubled—trebled— [aside to him.

Snob.

(aloud) No you don't. No bribery and corruption.

Tif.

I implore you to be silent. You shall become partner of the concern, if you please—only do not speak. You are not yourself at this moment. [aside to him.

Snob.

Ain't I though. I feel twice myself. I feel like two Snobsons rolled into one, and I'm choke full of the spunk of a dozen! Now Mr. Tiffany, Sir—

Tif.

I shall go distracted! Mr. Snobson, if you have one spark of manly feeling—[aside to him.

True.

Antony, why do you stand disputing with that drunken jackass? Where's your nigger? Let him kick the critter out, and be of use for once in his life.

Snob.

Better be quiet, Catteraugus. This ain't your hash, so keep your spoon out of the dish. Don't expose yourself, old boy.

True.

Turn him out, Anthony!

Snob.

He daren't do it! Ain't I up to him? Ain't he in my power? Can't I knock him into a cocked hat with a word? And now he's got my steam up—I will do it!

Tif.

(beseechingly) Mr. Snobson—my friend—

Snob.

It's no go—steam's up—and I don't stand at anything!

True.

You won't stand here long unless you mend your manners—you're not the first man I've upset because be didn't know his place.

Snob.

I know where Tiff's place is, and that's in the States' Prison! It's bespoke already. He would have it! He wouldn't take pattern of me, and behave like a gentleman! He's a forger, Sir!

[Tiffany throws himself into a chair in an attitude of despair; the others stand transfixed with astonishment.

He's been forging Dick Anderson's endorsements of his notes these ten months. He's got a couple in the bank that will send him to the wall any how—if he can't make a raise. I took them there myself! Now you know what he's worth. I said I'd expose him, and I have done it!

Mrs. Tif.

Get out of the house! You ugly, little, drunken brute, get out! It's not true. Mr. Trueman, put him out; you have got a stick—-put him out!

Enter Seraphina, L., in her bonnet and shawl—a parasol in her hand.

Sera.

I hope Zeke hasn't delivered my note.

[stops in surprise at seeing the persons assembled.

Mrs. Tif.

Oh, here is the Countess! [advances to embrace her.

Tif.

(starting from his seat, and seizing Seraphina violently by the arm) Are—you—married?

Sera.

Goodness, Pa, how you frighten me! No, I'm not married, quite.

Tif.

Thank heaven.

Mrs. Tif.

(drawing Seraphina aside, L.) What's the matter? Why did you come back?

Sera.

The clergyman wasn't at home—I came back for my jewels—the Count said nobility couldn't get on without them.

Tif.

I may be saved yet! Seraphina, my child, you will not see me disgraced—ruined! I have been a kind father to you—at least I have tried to be one—although your mother's extravagance made a madman of me! The Count is an impostor—you seemed to like him—(pointing to SNOBSON) Heaven forgive me! (aside) Marry him and save me. You, Mr. Trueman, you will be my friend in this hour of extreme need—you will advance the sum which I require—I pledge myself to return it. My wife—my child—who will support them were I—the thought makes me frantic! You will aid me? You had a child yourself.

True.

But I did not sell her—it was her own doings. Shame on you, Antony! Put a price on your own flesh and blood! Shame on such foul traffic!

Tif.

Save me—I conjure you—for my father's sake.

True.

For your father's son's sake I will not aid you in becoming a greater villain than you are!

Ger.

(C.) Mr. Trueman—Father, I should say—save him—do not embitter our happiness by permitting this calamity to fall upon another—

True.

Enough—I did not need your voice, child. I am going to settle this matter my own way.

[Goes up to Snobson—who has seated himself and fallen asleep—tilts him out of the chair.

Snob.

(waking up) Eh? Where's the fire? Oh! it's you, Catteraugus.

True.

If I comprehend aright, you have been for some time aware of your principal's forgeries?

[as he says this, he beckons to Howard, C., who advances as witness.

Snob.

You've hit the nail, Catteraugus! Old chap saw that I was up to him six months ago; left off throwing dust into my eyes—

True.

Oh, he did!

Snob.

Made no bones of forging Anderson's name at my elbow.

True.

Forged at your elbow? You saw him do it?

Snob.

I did.

True.

Repeatedly?

Snob.

Re—pea—ted—ly.

True.

Then you, Rattlesnake, if he goes to the States' Prison, you'll take up your quarters there too. You are an accomplice, an accessory!

[Truemanwalks away and seats himself, R. Howard rejoins Gertrude. Snobsob stands for some, time bewildered.

Snob.

The deuce, so I am! I never thought of that! I must make myself scarce. I'll be off! Tif, I say Tif! (going up to him and speaking confidentially) that drunken old rip has got us in his power. Let's give him the slip and be off. They want men of genius at the West,—we're sure to get on! You—you can set up for a writing master, and teach copying signatures; and I—I'll give lectures on temperance!

You won't come, eh? Then I'm off without you. Goodbye, Catteraugus! Which is the way to California? [steals off, L.

True.

There's one debt your city owes me. And now let us see what other nuisances we can abate. Antony, I'm not given to preaching, I therefore I shall not say much about what you have done. Your face speaks for itself,—the crime has brought its punishment along with it.

Tif.

Indeed it has, Sir! In one year I have lived a century of misery.

True.

I believe you, and upon one condition I will assist you—

Tif.

My friend—my first, ever kind friend,—only name it!

True.

You must sell your house and all these gew gaws, and bundle your wife and daughter off to the country. There let them learn economy, true independence, and home virtues, instead of foreign follies. As for yourself, continue your business—but let moderation, in future, be your counsellor, and let honesty be your confidential clerk.

Tif.

Mr. Trueman, you have made existence once more precious to me! My wife and daughter shall quit the city to-morrow, and—

Pru.

It's all coming right! It's all coming right! We'll go to the county of Catteraugus.

[walking up to Trueman.

True.

No you won't,—I make that a stipulation, Antony; keep clear of Catteraugus. None of your fashionable examples there!

Jolimaitre appears, L. H. 3 E., in the Conservatory and peeps into the room unperceived.

Count.

What can detain Seraphina? We ought to be off!

Mil.

(turns round, perceives him, runs and forces him into the room) Here he is!. Ah, Gustave, mon cher Gustave! 1 have you now and we never part no more. Don't frown, Gustave, don't frown—

True.

Come forward, Mr. Count! and for the edification of fashionable society confess that you're an impostor.

Count.

An impostor? Why, you abominable old—

True.

Oh, your feminine friend has told us all about it, the cook—the valet—barber and all that sort of thing. Come, confess, and something may be done for you.

Count.

Well, then, I do confess I am no count; but really, ladies and gentlemen, I may recommend myself as the most capital cook.

Mrs. Tif.

Oh, Seraphina!

Sera.

Oh, Ma! [they embrace and retire up.

True.

Promise me to call upon the whole circle of your fashionable acquaintances with your own advertisements

and in your cook's attire, and I will set you up in business to-morrow. Better turn stomachs than turn heads!

Mil.

But you will marry me?

Count.

Give us your hand, MIllinette! Sir, command me for the most delicate pati—the daintiest croquette ` la royale—the most transcendent omelette soufflie that ever issued from a French pastry-cook's oven. I hope you will pardon my conduct, but I heard that in America, where you pay homage to titles while you profess to scorn them—where Fashion makes the basest coin current—where you have no kings, no princes, no nobility—

True.

Stop there! I object to your use of that word. When justice is found only among lawyers—health among physicians—and patriotism among politicians, then may you say that there is no nobility where there are no titles! But we have kings, princes, and nobles, in abundance—of Nature's stamp, if not of Fashion's,—we have honest men, warm hearted and brave, and we have women—gentle, fair, and true, to whom no title could add nobility.

Epilogue

Pru.

I told you so! And now you hear and see. I told you Fashion would the fashion be!

True.

Then both its point and moral I distrust.

Count.

Sir, is that liberal?

How.

Or is it just?

True.

The guilty have escaped!

Tif.

Is, therefore, sin made charming ? Ah! there's punishment within! Guilt ever carries his own scourge along.

Ger.

Virtue her own reward!

True.

You're right, I'm wrong.

Mrs. Tif.

How we have been deceived!

Pru.

I told you so.

Sera.

To lose at once a title and a beau!

Count.

A count no more, I'm no more of account.

True.

But to a nobler title you may mount, and be in time—who knows?— an honest man!

Count.

Eh, Millinette?

Mil.

Oh, oui,—I know you can!

Ger.

(to audience) But, ere we close the scene, a word with you,—

We charge you answer,—Is this picture true? Some little mercy to our efforts show, Then let the world your honest verdict know. Here let it see portrayed its ruling passion, And learn to prize at its just value—Fashion.

Disposition of the characters

R. Count. Millinette. Howard. Gertrude. Trueman.

Mrs. Tiffany. Tiffany. Seraphina. Prudence.

THE END.

CPSIA information can be obtained at www.ICGtesting.com
Printed in the USA
BVOW031405301112

306898BV00001B/2/P